D0385574

My Natural History

My Natural History
Simon Barnes

Illustrations by Emily Fox

First published in Britain in 2010 by
Short Books
3A Exmouth House
Pine Street
EC1R 0JH

10 9 8 7 6 5 4 3 2 1

A CIP catalogue record for this book
is available from the British Library.

ISBN 978-1-906021-77-1

Printed in Great Britain by Clays
Cover design: Emily Fox

This one's for Ralph, with thanks for some wild times...
and for CLW as always

Contents

1. Greater horseshoe bat
Rhinolophus ferrumequinum

The animal kingdom came to my rescue. It always has done. I suspect it always will. It rescued me at Sunnyhill Primary School, it rescued me in my adolescence, it has rescued me over and over again throughout my adult life. The first, and perhaps the greatest rescue came when the animals rescued me from Mrs Watson, and at the same time, from Peter Miller, Raymond Stapleton and Philip Cunningham. It was the animals that rescued me from all the weariness and misery that Sunnyhill Primary School was able to provide. It was the animals that gave me hope. Animals have also given me sadness, profound distress, even despair: what do you expect? Love is always more complicated than you bargained for.

But first, to Mrs Watson and Sunnyhill. She was the headmistress. She was brutal, sadistic and mocking, and she hated me with all the delight of a nature rich in the talent for loathing. Not that I was alone. Among the many others she hated was Peter Miller, which should have made for a bond between us, but it didn't. If anything, it made him more eager for my chastisement. What Mrs Watson liked were well-behaved girls who sat at the front of the class; Susan Knight and Zoe Wright (for the latter of whom I had a small passion) basked in her favour. She also liked cheerful, manly little lads, boys who were neither dunces nor swots, good at football, loud, and popular: people like Peter Renvoize and Robert Faulkner. She didn't care for disruptive pupils from the meaner streets of Streatham; she cared even less for pupils with even the mildest pretensions to a more exotic background. Peter Miller and I represented two extreme forms of her disapproval.

Perhaps you think that I am making Mrs Watson too much of an ogre: that I am too eager to dramatise my run-of-the-mill childhood troubles. Believe me, Mrs Watson would be a remarkable figure now: perhaps she was even then. She consistently mocked a girl who wore a hearing aid. She was brutal to Michael Coleman, who failed to live up to her ideals of manliness. He attended Nancy Robinson School of Dance in Streatham High Road, the only boy from Sunnyhill to do so. He preferred to spend playtime gossiping with the girls: "Go out and play football with the boys!" Mrs Watson would bellow. He became a principal dancer with the Royal Ballet.

Sunnyhill School's catchment area was, in those days, mostly the domain of the least pretentious kind of middle class (a category that did not include my lot, of course) with a good sprinkling of working class, in days when such distinctions were reasonably clear, at least to grown-ups. There was one black boy in our class; he was universally popular. Even Mrs Watson tolerated him. My class had 45 pupils. Mrs Holland was our class teacher; she followed Mrs Watson's tastes but lacked her single-minded approach to the extortion of pain and misery.

Again, don't think I exaggerate. I remember an occasion when Peter Miller incurred Mrs Watson's displeasure, as he did on a regular basis, this time by running about on the tops of the desks. He was summoned to her room: he emerged with half a dozen weals across his calves. I remember the shock of seeing them: he had been beaten with genuine savagery. He was perhaps nine at the time, and seemed genuinely indifferent to it all. Perhaps he was used to far worse things. All the same, the stuff Mrs Watson got up to every week would be a newspaper scandal and a sacking offence today.

For her, humiliation was not a whim but an addiction. I remember the time Mr Gray denied her. I could sense the danger even then. He stood up to her at Assembly, in front of the whole school, in a manner I'll never forget; after all, it was me, among others, he was standing up for. It was his painful duty to report on an away match played by the school chess team, of which I was a member. The dozen of us were called to our feet before the whole school while Mr Gray delivered his match report. This was no pleasure. I had been beaten in three moves: the sequence known as Fool's Mate. I wasn't alone: the same horrible fate befell three or four of us. Mr Gray explained that the team had been soundly beaten: but that it was all his fault. He should have taught us Fool's Mate and how to guard against it. Mrs Watson's response was characteristic: "Oh, show us the fools!" she demanded, with great heartiness.

"No, I won't do that," Mr Gray said. "I think they all feel bad enough already." I could have kissed him. I certainly recognised a man of both courage and principle. He left soon after that. Mrs Watson was furious at this act of defiance: but then she was always furious: "I am exceedingly angry," she would boast, most days, when she led Assembly. If she had an aim as a teacher beyond humiliation, it was teaching the recorder. She had a passionate belief that every child should play the damn things; it was the sole route to salvation. In sporadic pursuit of this principle, she would sometimes invade a classroom, interrupt a lesson and force everyone to start blowing. The problem here is that she was a dreadful teacher. I never understood what she was on about, and nor did many others: we were rendered deaf and blind through terror. But I was the one who incurred her wrath that day, and it was dreadful. Even now, as a grown-up, though I love early music, especially when played on period instruments, I still prefer a flute to a recorder.

It was a recorder lesson that won me promotion from considerable dislike to pure hatred, though I think promotion was always coming. The problem was that I didn't fit in. Nor did my two sisters. We weren't a proper Streatham family, we had no roots there, we only landed there because we had been evicted by the Church of England. They needed our flat in Pimlico for their own purposes, and chucked out parents and three children between three and seven with a month's notice. Streatham saved us, but it wasn't our place. It wasn't that we were rich. But my father had worked in the theatre and then in television; my mother was a writer and lecturer. So when it came to assimilation, I didn't have much going for me. I was hopeless at sport, undersized, from the wrong social class, and was rather too prone to seek refuge in tears.

When she came into the class with a box of recorders, I knew no good could come from it. We were each issued with one of these things – instruments of torture rather than music – and were shown how to play a sequence of notes. I was at the back of the class, couldn't hear, couldn't understand, so I faked it earnestly. But then came the time of judgement: each pupil was required to play the notes as a solo. Zoë Wright and Susan Knight performed perfectly, because they already "did" the recorder. But soon, far too soon, it was my turn. I hadn't the remotest clue what to do. Under the terrifying eyes of Mrs Watson, I broke down. Tears overwhelmed me: tears of confusion and embarrassment and humiliation. Bad tactic. It led to a long lecture on the recorder, on failure, and the way to deal with failure. Having raised tears, Mrs Watson was eager to keep them flowing. She liked to spin things out. Eventually she concluded: what I should have said was "Sorry, I can't manage it". Bobby Hawkes was the next one asked to play: "Sorry, I can't manage it," he said. It was a betrayal. Or it felt like one: I can't really blame him for saving his own skin. So on around the class we went: one or two brave pupils essaying a few notes, most uttering the magic formula while, now apparently the sole failure, I sobbed harder and harder. This led to more and many hard words. At last the lesson ended. My humiliation was over.

Ah, but it wasn't, you see. The following day at Assembly, Mrs Watson was Exceedingly Angry. She told the story of the lesson, the recorder and the tears, my abject failure to say that I was sorry, I couldn't manage it. Before the entire school, I was held up as an example of the worst possible kind of human being: the sort of person we must all try, at all costs, not to be like. The entire school was, in short, given a licence for contempt: and my schoolmates accepted this gift with a glorious delight. Mrs

Watson hadn't mentioned my name, out of an elephantine delicacy. But my 44 class colleagues had no difficulty in penetrating the anonymity: and so by playtime, I was an object of derision for the whole school. It wasn't a great playtime: but playtimes were frequently the worst part of the day.

Peter Miller was a soft touch compared to Mrs Watson. All the same, he, Phillip Cunningham and Raymond Stapleton saw it as a duty to beat me up at playtimes on a regular basis. Now as physical punishment, things never went too far: it was all chasing and shoving and biffing, rather than the tortures of the Gestapo. It was merely an exercise in humiliation: I wonder where they got the idea from. The game was about raising tears: and tears were wrong, as Mrs Watson said, so I was wrong and they were right. I was fair game: even I had to admit that.

Sunnyhill School made at least one thing very clear to me: that if I was to do anything interesting with my life, it could only be done outside the school. Neither the lessons nor the social life offered inspiration. But I had the answer: I was mad about animals and birds. I read books, I went to the National History Museum at every opportunity. Picture me, back in those days of innocence, those days before paedophiliaphobia, when, aged nine or ten, I would catch the 49 bus from Streatham Common and get off at South Kensington. There I would walk the few hundred well-loved, well-walked yards through the tunnel to the

15

glorious façade of the museum: London's and the world's great temple to Life. And I would gaze at Diplodocus, gaze at the still bigger blue whale, look with wonder at the Diorama of African Game. I was never tired of the place, never bored when I was there. Every visit produced new wonders and old favourites. It was here, not at Sunnyhill, that I was educated.

Strange to relate, Robert Faulkner sometimes came with me. He was inspired by a school radio programme called *How Things Began*. I liked it myself, even though I knew most of it already: it was strange to find these glorious facts and these beloved extinct beasts in a place as alien as Sunnyhill. Naturally, Robert liked the dinosaurs. His mind was captivated by them, and what's more, he could draw them. I couldn't; I was hopeless. So he and I resolved to create the definitive book on dinosaurs: I would do the words, he the pictures. He would borrow a canvas stool from the place from which canvas stools could, for the deposit of a shilling, be borrowed, and he would sit on it and sketch dinosaurs while I rambled about and learned. Then we would have jelly with Carnation evaporated milk in the café at sixpence for a bowl and catch the 49 bus home. Life really was like that, back then.

I knew more about animals than any one in the school, largely because no one else cared. I remember explaining to Mrs Watson, in the naïve belief that through this knowledge I might win her respect, that a certain seashell on the school Nature Table was a univalve. (Univalves have a single entrance, like a snail or a whelk; bivalves are hinged and have a notional two doors, like an oyster or a mussel.) "Oh no," she said. "I think you'll find that's not a univalve." I thought then that there must be a kind of shell I didn't know about. There wasn't, of course; the bogus correction was just a way of humiliating me on my chosen subject.

Now there were times at Sunnyhill when I was accepted by this group or that group, but these periods never lasted long. There were many playtimes when my first priority was to escape from Peter Miller. About eight years later, I met him again. By this time I was dressed in full proto-hippy regalia: long hair, flared trousers, no doubt beads as well. Peter Miller was a skinhead, dressed in the then-modish parody of working-man's clothes: hair so short he was more or less bald, braces holding his trousers a considerable distance above an enormous pair of Doc Marten boots. We were on opposite sides of Valley Road, within a hundred yards of Sunnyhill. "You're Simon Barnes!" he shouted. I turned and penetrated the disguise of age and sectarian affiliation. He was unmistakably my former tormentor. "Peter Miller!" I think I had a notion of a road-crossing, a handshake, maybe a half-embrace: an agreement that a lot of water had flowed under a lot of bridges, that across time and social class and different 60s orientations, we would make some kind of rapport.

Peter Miller shouted: "Cunt!"

My second priority at playtime was to avoid everybody else. So I would go out into the wild world. And I became a bat-spotter, crawling through a fantastic cave system to find these strange and incomprehensible (to all save me) little mammals. My cave was in fact a tree, a sycamore that spread generously over the asphalt of the playground. I gazed up into its limestone branches, spotting bat after bat, unaware that you mostly find them in species-specific roosts. Ah, there was a pipistrelle, of course. And surely that was a noctule bat. And that one with the glorious little face and the absurd ears was a long-eared bat. And here was a lesser, and alongside, my favourite, a greater horseshoe bat: sublimely, quite beautifully ugly. Who in the school, who in the world save me, knew that its facial decoration was a noseleaf, and that its function was to amplify ultrasonic calls?

It was in such places I found myself whenever times were hard at Sunnyhill. Oh, not hard as many people know it: it was hardly Dickensian. Mrs Watson never hit me: no doubt she had more sense than to try it on with boys with middle-class parents. Or maybe she knew she didn't need to. No matter. She was a vile woman: but I was able to rise above her. The point is not my childish tribulations; but that I was able to soar away from them on the wings of a greater horseshoe bat. The bats, the shells, the dinosaurs, all the billion billion creatures that had ever populated the earth and my imagination – I didn't come to them because I needed consolation in hard times. I already had them. The refuge they provided from the Watsons and the Millers of this world was just a bonus. I didn't turn to wildlife because I was bullied and oppressed, I turned to wildlife out of love, and love helped me in a bad time, as love will. But love is far more than comfort. I was to learn that lesson more thoroughly as time passed, but I already knew the basics. There was more than mere escape here: there was also meaning, purpose, beauty and, especially, love. I reached these things through the power of the wild world and through the power of my imagination. And so far as I was concerned, the two things were indivisible.

2. Indri
Indri indri

Mr Gray wasn't my favourite teacher. I only saw him for things like Chess Club and School Play. But there were other wonderful teachers, and their mark is on me. S Vere Benson, for example. Not that I ever met her. But hers is a name that rings for ever in the minds of bird-watchers of a certain age. She wrote *The Observer's Book of Birds*, and for years, it was the only readily obtainable book of bird identification. It was first published in 1937, sold three million copies and had a shelf-life of half a century. It originally cost half a crown, or 12.5p if you must; by the time my father bought me mine, it was five shillings or 25p. I treasured it like a Gutenberg bible, finger pondered it nightly until I knew it by heart. It was the essential book in my life. Every illustration was like a revelation of the divine vision. By the time I was ten, I had to buy a new copy, because I read the old one to bits.

I was always poor at arithmetic; my natural ineptitude combined with the teaching of Mrs Holland was a fatal combination. It was decided at home that I must "learn my tables"; that is to say, to get the multiplication tables by heart. My father wrote them out for me in his speculative italic hand, and I duly learned them. I still know them: if you ever want to know what nine eights are, you have only to ask. It was a triumph of corruption: I pulled off this feat because I had been bribed. I was entitled to choose any book in the world, other than, I suppose, a Gutenberg bible. I acquired something far more precious: *A Field Guide to the Birds of Britain and Europe* by Roger Tory Peterson, Guy Mountfort and PAD Hollom: a trio of teachers that made me forget Mrs Watson and all her works.

I read this to shreds also. It had far more birds than *The Observer's Book*: nearly three times as many. S Vere Benson described 243; Roger Tory Peterson and his pals told me about a mind-spinning 500-plus, and then went on to talk about more than 100 accidentals. So many birds! Birds and birds and birds: I had not thought life had created so many. I knew about buzzard, of course, "easily recognised by its mewing cry"; and S Vere had mentioned rough-legged buzzard in a throwaway paragraph. But now I could learn about honey buzzard and long-legged buzzard as well, and pore over many pictures of every species: so many buzzards! So many different kinds of legs! And how could anyone tell these buzzards from Bonelli's eagle and booted eagle and short-toed eagle? How could you see an eagle's toes? I knew about golden eagle: but now I had to wonder: was imperial eagle still better? I mused on the question night after night, turning the pages. I thought I was learning about birds: in truth, I was, for the first time, beginning an understanding of a subject that in those days didn't even have a name. Despite that, it had me enthralled then, as it has enthralled me all my life. I was learning the greatest lesson of my life, and it was not arithmetic and not the recorder. The name of the subject is biodiversity.

Those accidentals, they were the most marvellous thing of all. Time and again, I would turn to the terse paragraph that described wandering albatross *Diomedea exulans*: "Largest ocean bird (11 ft wing-span). Mainly white, black wing-tips..." Imagine that. Imagine seeing one. And imagine I did: my imagination was haunted by birds, and particularly the wandering albatross. In the *Field Guide*, all the birds described fully and illustrated had been "officially recorded" in Europe at least 20 times. An accidental was, I learned, a bird that had made even fewer appearances. In other words, it was very, very rare: so rare it hardly existed. So rare it was almost a myth. It was a bird that nobody would ever see, a bird of the imagination. Naturally, I looked for the wandering albatross all the time: off the shore at Southsea and Paignton, but without any expectation at all of seeing one. I just looked out and imagined: and look! There it was! Coming in past the pier, or perhaps cruising over from Torquay, a nonchalant master of the winds and the waves, banking with airy grace on its giant wings, and I alone was there to understand. But I don't think it was the glory of seeing one that really mattered to me. It was the glory of being one. I too was an albatross, I too was an Accidental, I too was a rare being, I too was to be treasured in my wandering isolation.

Rare, rare. The more precious because rare: the more precious because so few. I hadn't grasped the point that albatrosses are rarely seen in Britain and Europe because their heartland is the Southern Ocean; that their only reason for coming so far north is, indeed, accidental. The poor things only come here when they get lost. But I preferred the idea of a mighty bird of devastating fragility: a magnificent warlord in need of protection: a vulnerable conquistador: a glorious oxymoron. I believed that there were just a few lone birds sadly and patiently working the endless seas on their enormous wings: unicorns with feathers, birds that told us humans of better times, long-lost times when there were more beautiful things than we could ever imagine.

I had other teachers too. Gerald Durrell ripped away the solemnity of the birdy text books, and their traditionally awful prose, and never thought for a second that jokes compromised love, still less reverence. I read all his books, many of them many times. Television brought untold wonders right into the sitting room in Streatham. Peter Scott presented a programme called *Look* which seemed to be broadcast for me alone. Everything he said, everything he showed me had an added vividness because I knew the story of Scott and the nene, the Hawaiian goose brought back from extinction by the Wildfowl Trust. Imagine doing such a thing – and imagine I did. Savour the words: the rarest goose in the world. It is found – and I loved that slip into the passive voice, that technique beloved of serious bird books, something that seemed to imply a strange and portentous mystery, as it indeed did – only in Hawaii. By 1952, the wild population was down to 30. Then Scott took a hand and started a captive breeding programme at the headquarters of his Wildfowl Trust in Slimbridge, Gloucestershire. This led to a successful re-release programme: and there are now about 500 wild nenes honking their stuff – their name is an onomatopoeia – about Hawaii.

When I left Sunnyhill, I got a prize. So did almost everybody except Peter Miller, so far as I remember. I got, for we were allowed to choose, *Zoo Quest for a Dragon*, by, of course, David Attenborough. I have it on my shelves still, so I can remind myself that in 1962, it was presented to me for Attainment and Good Work In English. (Attainment meant getting a place in a Good School.) The book contains Attenborough's signature, because my father knew him from his work at the BBC. I read the book and enjoyed it: but it was the pride of possession that was the main thing. It was Attenborough's television performances that overwhelmed me. It was not just the fabulous places and the fabulous beasts: it was the fact that he really cared. You could see him caring. You could see him not faking it. He cared like I cared. Here was a grown-up who thought it really mattered that an animal should live rather than die. It was as if Attenborough gave me permission to care. Attenborough told me that my anguish and my joy in the wild world had a real value: that love of the wild was not something you grew out of.

There was one series in particular. It was the series of 1961, *Zoo Quest to Madagascar*. The details are vague in my memory, but I remember the awful, the beautiful anxiety as Attenborough hunted for a lemur that had never before been filmed. It was a revelation of the terrible fragility of the wild world: the first time that such an idea had struck me. Not that the programme dealt with the threat of extinction, for Attenborough was never one for scare stories, never one for going off half-cock. It was some years later that the accumulating weight of evidence made him the most forceful and vivid campaigner for the endangered wild on the entire planet. But for me at least, there was a strange presentiment of this future orthodoxy in the story of the indri, in this tale of a great man, the best possible substitute for me, travelling round a wild and remote place in an apparently hopeless quest for a strange and lovely creature that nobody had heard of and nobody could find.

Years later, years and years later, I met Attenborough when we were both doing some work for the conservation charity, the World Land Trust. I was taking drinks, as good conservationists do when business is over, in the glorious double-decker library of the Linnean Society in Piccadilly, and as extraordinary coincidence would have it, I found myself by the table with the drink on it, clutching a bottle. I turned to find Attenborough with an empty glass beside me, so I filled it. As a result I was able to ask a question that had been troubling me for years: "What was the lemur? The one you tried so hard to find and thought you never would?"

I had wondered if my description and my memory were too vague. But not a bit of it. There was only one possibility: "Indri!" And a flood of reminiscence and anecdote, wonderfully told over a diminishing glassful: Attenborough is as great a performer for one as he is for millions. It was, and still is, a question of caring about the subject. It was, and always is, a question of love. Attenborough was, and for that matter, still is, my favourite teacher.

Indri! The biggest surviving lemur, weighing up to 29 pounds, a teddy-faced jumper with a taste for music: the great singer of the Malagasy forests. Lemurs are primates, like us: one of the earliest forms in which our group took shape. They were out-competed on mainland Africa by monkeys and apes (like ourselves) but they somehow got to Madagascar after it had separated from the African mainland and set about a great adaptive radiation. Presumably the pioneers got there by rafting, by getting lifts across the strait – accidental lifts – on tumbled and floating vegetation. There the lemurs ceased to be losers and became winners: virtuosi of evolution, creating more and more new species to fill one niche after the next: from extinct giants to tiny little things like the pygmy mouse lemur, from lemurs that live much as monkeys do, to the aye-aye that sneaks about in the dark and thinks it's a woodpecker. (It has a middle finger three times the length of the others and pokes it into holes in tree trunks for larvae.) The name lemur is from the Latin; *lemures* are spirits of the night. Perhaps it is the haunting song of the indri that prompted this name. It is a sound I have never heard in person, and it is as strange a din as nature has come up with. The indri is something of a tree-bound whale.

And I revelled in Attenborough's search for the indri: the elusive, the near-lost, the all-but-unfindable beast, the myth of the Malagasy forests. But he found it: wonder of wonders, he found it, and there he was, in black-and-white images caught on a clockwork camera, brought to our sitting room, brought even to the postal district of SW16.

Surely, I thought, it is a wild world out there, a world in which wonderful things exist, but one in which they can't take anything for granted.

All was not as it should be in this world. I knew that after the search for the indri. I knew then that it was not possible to love the wild world without knowing pain. Though Attenborough found his indri, I knew that it might just as easily have come out the other way: almost, I could see him on television apologising for the fact that he had been unable to find an indri, that there weren't enough indris to find. And this would not have been an admission of a failure of the human ability to find things: it would have been an admission of a failure of the human ability to keep things. To look after things. I knew that if I chose to continue loving wildlife, I would be choosing a way in which sadness was unavoidable. And I embraced it willingly.

3. Beadlet anemone
Actinia equina

It troubled me that I didn't love the sea. Such loving was required behaviour. It was essential that I loved Cornwall with a deep and special passion, and that meant loving the sea. Cornwall was the land of our holidays: family all together, father not at the BBC, mother not writing or lecturing, school forgotten. It was the land of treats and everything could only ever be marvellous. To believe anything else would be an unthinkable crime; worse, a kind of blasphemy. But I swam poorly, and the Cornish seas, even in August, sucked the warmth and, it seemed, the life from my body. Most of my encounters with the sea involved brief immersion followed by agonies of teeth-chattering.

Nick was different. Nick, son of my parents' close friends, had a light covering of adipose tissue, but despite this, was athletic and courageous. He never felt the cold, and swam in the sea for endless hours, completely at home in its icy embrace. He revelled in every second: he was every parent's ideal of how a boy should enjoy Cornwall. I envied the approval he won with his exploits: envied him, to an extent, the pleasures he found in the water. I used to tell him that he was a seal. He really did look like a seal, but in truth, he was a human supremely adapted for the aquatic life in a hard climate.

We went daily to Rinsey Beach, descending the dizzying cliff path with swimming things and picnic baskets, hours later making the long and wearisome stomp back up again, Nick pleasantly fatigued from his congress with the waves, me exhausted from hours of shivering. As you looked down, you could see the rock pools that punctuated the beach: ancient cracks and fissures flushed and refilled twice a day with the advancing and retreating tides. They were limpet-lined, a strange unexpected shade of pink below the surface, weed-hung, and decorated with sea anemones. They were strange, alien places, more unlike Streatham than anything it was possible to encounter. These pools were my favourite thing about Cornwall, but I was, of course, an outsider, a mere gazer-in. And not just with rock pools: most of nature was like that for me, either imagined, or just a little beyond my scope.

Now Nick, having wealthy parents, wanted for very little. He was also deeply generous and would lend you anything. So one day I borrowed his snorkel. I don't know what possessed me to do this. It just seemed a nice toy. In those days, very few people visited Rinsey, and most of those that did were known to us. Because of this, we were able to make our camp in the same place every day, in front of the same rock pool, one in which both my sisters learned to swim. So that morning, I entered it, not without that terrible gasp when the water rises above your crotch, but I endured this hardship, being cautiously in the mood for adventure. I placed the mask over my face. It was an old-fashioned, one-piece snorkel: a tube rising from the mask itself, so if you breathed through your nose, you could continue with your face submerged. I was nervous of it: the act of putting your face under water and then breathing does, after all, go against nature.

First I tried to place the mask in the water without getting my whole face wet. This was an instant and dramatic shock, making me gasp and pull my head up again. It wasn't the breathing that shocked, but the seeing. The transformation was extraordinary. The vista revealed by the second-long glance was no longer a blurry, shifting, distorted mess of colour: it was a clearly-seen world of hard edges and living, breathing things. It invited me in with a seduction so intense that gasping was inevitable. It was almost as if the water had turned warm.

It took a few tries before I was able to do the actual breathing, and a few more before I was able to swim and breathe at the same time. But swim I did: at once transforming myself from an inadequate water-shy human to a great hovering bird, gliding above a vast landscape, looking down benignly on crabs and sudden, scuttling blennies. At once the remote became near: the foreign became familiar: the separate became unity. Nature, wild things, me: we were all the same thing. That day I lifted my head from the pool only to eat and to shiver. I had found my love.

Cornwall was wild; Streatham, for the most part, was tame. Cornwall was where we went in search of wildness. True, finding actual wildlife was not at the top of everybody's agenda: or not knowingly. That was as true for me as it was for everybody else. But certainly, we went there in order to be surrounded by nature. We sought reasons to believe in the total and utter specialness of Cornwall and of Rinsey, and everything that confirmed this was a joy, from the casual mastery of the seagulls to the emerald lights of the glow-worms along the cliff path.

My mother had a special love for the choughs that thronged the cliffs, tumbling in the wind and calling "Jack! Jack!" to each other. It will be clear here, at least to the birdwatchers among my readers, that my mother's sense of what was appropriate was more sharply honed than her powers of observation. At the time, choughs were extinct in Cornwall, surviving only on the county coat of arms. The bird had long been part of Cornish life, and was still part of Cornish folklore, but it was no longer there in flying and nesting reality. It was jackdaws that stall-turned and barrel-rolled in the updraughts along the cliffs.

My mother loved being in Cornwall more than anywhere else, with the family together and harmonious, and partaking of ritual meals together on a nightly basis, and with friends constantly coming round for food and drink and laughter. Cornwall's specialness mattered to her even more than it did to the rest of us: she, I think, set the tone for specialness. But her choughs were the choughs of imagination.

With the dead, there is an eternal regret that you can't tell them things any more, or show them things. I can't show my mother my children and her grandchildren; I can't show her this book; I can't show her choughs. For it is a matter of sweet sadness that the choughs came back to Cornwall a dozen years after she died. It is a strange and deeply cheering tale. A number of farmers had been persuaded, with financial inducements, to manage cliff-top land in a manner sympathetic to choughs, for choughs traditionally feed on rough pastures near the sea in frost-free places. Cornwall lost many of its rough pastures when farmers took to tractors and no longer needed horses for farm work. Once these pastures were re-established, the plan was to release captive-bred birds and see what happened. But before this could take place, the choughs came back by themselves. As I write, there are half a dozen pairs and family groups, and one of these is regularly seen about Rinsey. I remember the extraordinary pleasure I had in seeing them for the first time: deeply black birds with fire-red beaks and legs, flying together in family groups in the big cliff-top winds, looking like a handful of old dusters. And they don't say "Jack!". Instead they give out a long drawled "chooooow!". It was the voice, one I had heard a few times elsewhere, that drew me to them first: and in disbelief. I found them with my binoculars and waited till the sun caught their legs and their redness to give me full certainty. They were choughs all right, but I couldn't tell my mother about them, and I regret very much the pleasure it would have given her: pleasure in the wildness, in the specialness, and perhaps above all, in the appropriateness. The Cornish chough was back in Cornwall.

But she did have one glorious and unforgettable bird-watching experience in Cornwall: and this from someone who was never a birdwatcher, had poor eyesight and was never much at good at observation of any kind. She was sitting by the window in the cottage in Cornwall, reading, or more probably, doing the *Times* crossword, for it was a disappointing day when she failed to complete it. She looked up, no doubt thinking of an anagram or a quotation, and saw a bird. And it took her breath away. At once, she was in a world of wonder and delight and disbelief. It was as if she had dived into my rock pool.

For the bird was a hoopoe. A hoopoe! How did she know this? I wonder. True, a hoopoe is remarkable and extraordinary and unmistakable: she must have come across the bird somehow in the course of her eternal task of reading. A hoopoe is the most exotic of occasional dropper-inners, salmon-pink, black-and-white wings, a huge and ridiculous crest, and a flight like a demented butterfly. It is the most eye-catching of birds, even in the places where it is common, and my mother's eye was well and truly caught. She rang me to tell me about it that evening, breathless in the excitement of the telling, saying, without a shred of irony: "It really was one of the most wonderful moments of my life."

All her life she had been caught up with the telling of tales: often recounting the lives of great humans for the children's television programme, *Blue Peter*. She liked cities. She had deep sentimental feelings about Rome. She loved to sit in that *campo* or this in Venice and take a glass of something cool and cheering as Venice performed for her benefit. But all her life, she had this nagging, scarcely understood nostalgia for wild things. After she had her first terrible stroke, she was filled with a thousand regrets, and one of the greatest of those was that she would never be able to go to Africa. She understood, too late in life, that this was something she had always longed to do. And I remembered Alice and the beautiful garden, the garden she can't get into because the key is on the table and she is too small to reach it. Alas, when she grows tall enough to reach the key, she is too big to get through the door and can only peer along the short passage to the place of perfection that lies beyond.

The entire wild world was like that for me, even in Cornwall: there, but just beyond my reach, just beyond my scope, just beyond my understanding. I remember my almost hoopoe-esque delight when a couple of gannets came close enough on shore to be seen with the naked eye, plunging crazily into the water with their spear-beaks. I remember a pair of common terns, diving as dizzily but somehow more daintily. I thought these were miraculous appearances: I know now that they are available for anyone with the desire to see, with the right understanding, with the knowledge of how to look. From Rinsey cliffs you can see terns passing by as a regular thing, and if you look out to sea, you often see distant gannets cruising the airways and, every now and then, swivelling on a wing-tip-tip to make a crazy-lethal plunge at the waters below.

Wildlife is like that for the unawakened. Sometimes it comes in a blinding hoopoe flash: but more often, you feel most dreadfully excluded. You have to find a way. You need to find a new way of seeing. It all adds up, eventually, to a new way of being. That is what I learned when I borrowed Nick's snorkel: but it took me years to learn that this lesson had a meaning far beyond rock pools. Meanwhile, I looked at sea anemones and wished that

Streatham was wilder, not knowing that the main fault was not with Streatham but with my seeing, my being.

4. Great northern diver
Gavia immer

I went to my big school, and was rewarded for my attainment in getting there. I was liked. I was popular. I was, in a narrow kind of way, a success. But Lord, I was bored. I was so bored, I can't look back on those years – five of them – without a shudder. I got through them easily enough though. That's because I didn't realise I was bored. I just assumed that this was what life had to offer: that this was what it was supposed to be like.

I had friends, I always had friends. I had some really great friends. Stuart Barnett was as nice a fellow as anyone could hope to meet. We made a pair: we also made a trio with Ian Hart, whose attitude of fine contempt for everything to do with the idea of education for its own sake was shocking and exhilarating. But God, those days were dull.

It wasn't the fault of the days and it wasn't the fault of the friends. It was my own most grievous fault: and it came about because of my problems with such things as seeing and being.

I mustn't overdo the Stephen Dedalus stuff, or make too much of the different-from-other-boys line. There was no martyrdom, no persecution, no ill-will; for that matter, no thwarted artistry, no sense of destiny, still less of superiority. They were just years without passion: years without much meaning: years in limbo. Perhaps that is what this awkward period of life is supposed to be like: neither child nor man, not even a teenager, in any exacting sense of the term. I was just some one who did homework – we called it prep – and watched telly and made jokes about the teachers. A time of nothing: a time in life's waiting room.

My limited popularity initially went to my head. I was at Emanuel School; you can see it as you pass southwards from Clapham Junction, heading for either Wimbledon or Streatham: the line splits and passes either side of the school. There was a school review called *Between the Lines*. At the time, it was a lapsed public school, its clientele unrestrainedly middle class. I was no longer a misfit. The pupils of Emanuel were a great deal more like me than the pupils of Sunnyhill: but all the same, I wanted to be a great deal more like them than I was. I wanted to be a conformist, I wanted to be a fitter-inner. I wanted to have a place: and it seemed to me that the way to do this was by means of sport. There were disadvantages to this plan: the greatest of which was the fact that there was no sport that I was any good at. I was still undersized, physically insignificant; I did most of my growing later, in a great hurry, after every one else had stopped.

The school played rugby. I was determined to make my lack of size an advantage: I would be the most elusive runner the school had ever seen, or at least, the best in my class, or form, as we called it. But I lacked pace, I lacked physical resilience, I lacked the taste for manly encounters in the mud. I didn't care for tackling or being tackled, though in this I was hardly unique. After a couple of weeks' trial, I was a failure and sent off to play in the useless-buggers games while the half-decent players were trained up to represent the school. The games my lot played were awful. They were painful for the participants and they must have been agony for any of the teachers (masters, we called them) who actually cared about sport. No one cared who won. No one wanted to be out there in the cold and the mud. We only did it because there was no escape. No one tackled. The worst that might happen to a ball-carrier was to be seized in a half-hearted embrace. No one went to ground if it was at all avoidable: one of the objects of the game was to get as little mud on you as possible, and so avoid the post-match shower. Scrums were a torment: no one wanted to be in a hugger-buggering mass of 15 others, in serious danger of getting dirty. I was once, absurdly, sent to play hooker as punishment by our understandably frustrated captain. He thought I wasn't trying, and reader, he was right. I gleefully punted the ball into the opposition scrum every time it came to me.

We didn't have many good runners, but we were all great passers. There was always a danger of getting tackled, or at least embraced, if you happened to be carrying the ball, for the ball was like the black spot, the runes that were cast in the MR James story: a portent of doom unless you could somehow divert the furies onto someone else. It follows that one of the signature moves of these games was the pass into touch: if by some mischance you had the ball, and were forced to run with it, and then saw a decent-sized opponent ahead, you passed the ball, obviously. If there was no colleague in sight – and there was always a curious melting-away in the face of anyone who might be considering a proper tackle – you passed the ball over the white line and so avoided the dreaded embrace. We neither got fit nor enjoyed ourselves, nor fulfilled any useful function. If we learned team ethics it was in the shared desire to avoid anything that sport of this kind could offer. Those games have stayed in mind as the ultimate expression of the futility of those years: a game played for no reason, in which no victory was savoured and no defeat painful, in which none of the players desired anything except its conclusion.

On days when it was too wet to play rugby – mustn't spoil the grass – we were told to run around the field half a dozen times. Unexpectedly, I turned out to be rather good at that. Most people, even the rugby keenies, jogged three or four laps and then sloped off, because no one counted the laps; the whole process was an initiative test for cheats. The fatties merely walked a couple of laps, an admission of failure. But I was not only honest, after a fashion, I also liked running. I was fast and I never got tired. I used to enjoy running off the serious rugby players, and they didn't like that. But running didn't count: running couldn't be serious, if someone like me was good at it. Still, it was running that brought me my friendship with Stuart.

Stuart loved sport of all kinds and was naturally talented at everything he took up. He was school scrum-half; he was the wicket-keeper-batsman; in the brief athletics season, he was unbeatable. But he was never at all swanky about it. He just saw it as the natural turn of events. And he could run. He could run almost as well as me. One wet Thursday afternoon, I noticed him behind me, so naturally I resolved to run him off. I could run everyone off. But for once, I failed. Every time I looked back, there he was behind me: a lot of freckles, a pale ginger flop of hair and a challenging, but somehow unthreatening grin. He was enjoying the tussle: enjoying my discomfiture, enjoying the fact that at last, he had found someone to race.

I think I won that one, but no matter. We became friends, and sport was at the centre of it. True, I hated sport, but Stuart was so nice that this didn't matter. We formed a sort of sporting alliance, along with Ian, and every break, morning and lunchtime, we played football against Chris Ellis, Stuart Lloyd and Mick Moutrie. We played with a plastic ball with holes in, the only permitted kind, since balls like that didn't break windows. I was useless and I hated every minute of it. But it was good to do something I hated with people I liked. I was accepted.

We went to lessons, did our prep and we went up through the school. As we did so, our style changed by degrees. Our cropped or unruly hair evolved into carefully combed styles. Shoes that were used to dam streams were swapped for shoes of finicky elegance, though we still played football in them, my illegal elastic-sided shoes occasionally soaring skywards from my flailing feet. Collars were no longer frayed and twisted: we now wore exotic "tab" collars and button-downs. We put cuff-links in our shirts and wore our ties in a half-Windsor knot. Those that could grew side-whiskers while those of us that couldn't died of shame.

But there was still nothing I was interested in. Nothing I was passionate about. My love of the wild had been subsumed by my popularity, such as it was. Oh, I still read the books and watched the programmes, but the wild world was no longer the centre of my life. It seemed to me then that my passion for wildlife had, after all, been nothing more than consolation for unhappiness: something to grow out of. And swap for what? I had yet to learn that if the non-human world is a consolation in times of unhappiness, it is a lot of other things as well. Back then, though, in Upper Four Arts, there was no one to show me that the wild world offers joys, an endless store of questions, a wonder and a beauty that can improve the lot of the happiest person on earth. There was no one to share my passion for the wild. There was no Bird-Spotters Club, no Natural History Society, no Bug-Hunters. Instead, there was only conformism, the playing field, the quad and the ball that didn't break windows. It didn't seem enough, but I thought that was all there was.

So I joined the Boat Club. I was in search of prestige, in search of meaning. I wanted to make my size a serious sporting asset. I wanted to be upsides with Stuart in the sporting arena. So I became a cox. This was a terrible idea: the worst. The Boat Club saw itself as the natural home of the school's sporting elite. For some time before I joined, I scanned its notice board: not that it meant anything to me, but I loved the sense of self-belief that emanated from it, that sense of corporate identity. I longed to be a part of it. Eventually, I was. And I hated it.

I was the right size, true, but I had neither the gift of watermanship nor the taste for command. I also felt the cold bitterly. When we stopped for a session of talk from the bicycling coach who followed our haphazard progress from the towpath, the boat drifted alarmingly. My instructions for its righting were always panicky and ineffective. I never knew the wise course to steer. On more than one occasion I ran aground. I hit at least a couple of bridges, which is easier to do than you might think, though you have to put your mind to it. I once rammed another eight; another time I sent my boat and its hapless crew careering on a flooding tide into a moored motor-boat. In short, the Boat Club was a torment to me, and I was a torment to the Boat Club. Eventually, and rightly, they asked me to stop.

My enduring memory is the stink of the river. The Boat Club required my presence on Wednesday afternoons and Saturday mornings: I would arrive at Barnes Bridge Station and all but taste the vile effluence of the water. The stink of the Thames of the 1960s was the stink of a dying river: sweet Thames, run softly till I end my song. The smell was the smell of my failure: my failure to master the arts of coxswainship, my failure at sport, my failure to find anything in life that I cared about. And so I sat on the little wooden shelf at the back of the needle-shaped boat with eight larger boys in a line before me, them grasping the handles of their oars, me holding the wooden toggles attached to the rudder, and off we went, me steering another hellship to God knew where. Lessons and playground football and the riverine stink: and thank God, friendship. I thought then that this was life: all it had to

45

offer: a succession of one boring thing after another; a process in which you went through the motions, not really caring about what you were doing, in which neither victory nor defeat had any savour. Life had nothing to stir my blood.

I was standing at the boathouse, looking out at the river, when I saw it. A bird. That itself was enough to make it rare in those days. The river held very few birds, for it contained nothing to eat: the fish had been stunk out. But here was a big, big bird, and it was sitting low on the water, a cigar-shaped body, a bit of a neck (but not like a swan or a goose) and a long, sharp beak. I looked on it with astonishment: it could only be a diver. It was seriously big: that meant it had to be a great northern diver, the very first bird in *The Observer's Book of Birds*. I gazed at it in disbelief: there was me, and there was a genuinely rare bird: almost an Accidental.

As a point of information, I should say here that it wasn't a great northern diver. I know that now. It was a cormorant, seen from an unfamiliar angle and in an unfamiliar place. But that's not the point. The point is that I saw this thing of wonder: and I didn't know what the hell to do about it. I had no one to tell. No one would be interested, no one would care. It was outside the concerns of Emanuel School. Stuart would make a joke, a friendly but mocking one; Ian would make another, sharper, more destructive. So I never mentioned it to any one. I didn't know whether to be happy, whether to go home and look it up, whether to forget about it. Well, I didn't forget about it. The bird, the memory stayed with me. I knew it wasn't a joke, but I didn't know what it was, what it meant, how I was supposed to react. It wasn't a joking matter; but then it wasn't anything else, either.

It was like seeing the Holy Grail bobbing about in the river and watching it float by. Isn't that the meaning of life? Never mind, what have we got for prep? The thing I sought more than anything else in the world was already in plain view, and I did nothing. In this way, life, wild or tame, carries on. And so I went out and coxed the Colts A, brought them back for once unscathed, caught the train to Streatham, changing at Clapham Junction, wishing I had already done my prep. Wondering why life was so dull.

5. Adder
Vipera berus

He was pretty formidable. He had heavy black glasses, side-whiskers that reached his jawbone and an air of knowing what he was about in the world. We had never spoken: he came to Lower Six Arts by a different route. That's why I expected him to be a second-rater, but right from the start, it was clear that he had the sharpest mind in the history group, the only one of us with a proper grasp of the subject. He was in a different English group, but I gathered that he excelled there, too. So I was distinctly wary of him. It was he that spoke first, observing that I had come to school with an armful of LPs borrowed from the gramophone library in Streatham; I was planning to change them on the way home. I can't remember what the records were, probably Bach. We established that he too had a taste for music. He was especially fond of the Bartok string quartets. This was a bit beyond my scope, but I countered gamely with Scarlatti harpsichord sonatas.

His name was Ralph, rhyming with safe rather than Alf; though Ralph was never safe. He was the most dangerous boy in the school. I had no objection to that. Gradually, a new alliance was formed. I started to spend time with Ralph and his friend Ted. Ted was an artist's son, shock-haired, singular, with a mind that strove constantly for the bizarre. Radical politics became part of our conversation: here, Ralph was the leader. We let our hair grow. I abandoned cuff-links and tab-collars: I reverted to my first-form scruffiness, save that this state was now cultivated with dandified care. We affected illegalities of dress: Ralph had black flared (flared!) trousers worn with brown zipper boots; I had grey suede Chelsea boots.

It is accepted as a truism of history that the 60s were about pleasure and excitement, that all young people were on the same side, that everyone who lived through those turbulent years was part of it, out there on the cutting edge, having the time of his life, enjoying guilt-free pleasures, cultivating an exotic appearance, rebelling against outmoded traditions, establishing a new and vibrant future. But it is a flagrant lie. It wasn't like that at all. It was a time of polarisation: of bitter oppositions.

The strongest opponents of these burgeoning freedoms, this incipient rebellion, were our own classmates. It was not the masters but the prefects who lined up against us. They saw themselves as mature. They aped their elders. They dressed as smartly as possible. Most importantly, they sincerely believed that conformity was not a matter of taste and temperament but a moral obligation. My French group was asked to write an essay about the Anouilh play, *Antigone*, declaring whether we sided with Antigone and the forces of freedom and individuality, or Créon, conformity and obedience. Four of the class, all of them prefects, took Créon's side: so much for the wild 60s. They didn't know, or if knowing, didn't care, that the play was a coded examination of the polarities of Nazism and the French Resistance, and that Créon spoke for the Nazis.

I was in the forefront of the Sixth Form Resistance myself. Momentous things were happening in society: momentous things were happening to me. I too was taking part in a drama: I had a part, and it wasn't Créon. I had an identity. I wasn't bored. I read passionately, and Ralph and I talked books eternally: he was for Lawrence, I was for Joyce. Art mattered. For the others, art was just a subject useful for the passing of exams, we scoffed. We knew better. And when we walked through the school, people knew who we were. We were stars. I was no longer a reluctant football-player in a tab-collared shirt: no longer a third-rate imitation of the "mature" boys, the would-be prefects. No: I was a first-rate intellectual dissident – the best the school could come up with, anyway – with hair bouncing on my coat-collar. Ralph and I helped to set up a unilateral sixth-form council, a piece of insurrection that alarmed the headmaster and absolutely horrified the prefects. We were proposing democratically elected leaders instead of unilaterally appointed ones: this had to be stamped out, and was. Still, we had a fine old time stirring things up.

A moment of apotheosis. Ralph had pinned to the noticeboard an inflammatory document, calling on we the undersigned to condemn something or other: the way the school was run, or maybe the way the headmaster refused to speak against American intervention in Vietnam. The subject doesn't matter. What mattered was that the headmaster, Charles Kuper, elected to make the judgment of Voltaire. He made a fine speech before all the school, speaking about the freedoms a previous generation had fought for, and said that while he disagreed with the document, he would defend to the death our right to pin it to the wall.

"Why has it been taken down then?"

What? Interrupting the headmaster? Interrupting the headmaster in the middle of Assembly? Six hundred heads swivelled through 180 degrees and looked up at the gallery, the place sacred to the sixth form. In the very back row, shoulders against the wall, each with two feet on the chair in front, three wild and dangerous rebels: Ralph, the one who had spoken, long black curls like a judge's wig, dangerous glasses and those ferocious whiskers; Ted making the entire concept of uniforms and uniformity meaningless; me. And no, it wasn't a great moment of rebellion: rather, it was a great moment in the establishment of personal identity. We three: we rebels. (It turned out that the head prefect had taken the document down on his own initiative. He refused to return it, despite the headmaster's overt approval. He said it was undermining Authority. Never mind what the headmaster said: it was immoral and it had to go.)

Ralph became part of my family. He was always around our house, and was a great success with everyone. We established running jokes: Ralph is part of family folklore to this day. His sharpest remarks, his always exaggerated – so he claims – faux pas, his jokes crop up whenever two or three of the family are together. It was one of those friendships of early maturity that is almost like a love affair, but with all sensual elements removed. There is a greater intimacy in such a friendship than is ever found in the alliances of maturity. We knew each other's secrets. We knew each other's weaknesses. We knew all each other's jokes. We knew each other's embarrassments, each other's triumphs. We were, for a time, each other's completion: each other's validation.

Ralph started coming on holiday to Cornwall with us. We had been brought up to love the dramatic landscapes of that extraordinary place: but Ralph seemed to have a deeper and subtler understanding of it. It was not wildlife with him, not exactly. Rather it was the shape of the land itself that moved him: the sensation of the landscape as a narrative, as a tale still being told, as a place trodden by humans from one millennium to the next.

For our view of the world was changing. We no longer saw the way ahead as one of violent revolution. We weren't Marxists or Maoists any more. We were now impelled towards a romantic anarchy. We sought instead a revolution in thinking, a revolution in seeing the world, a revolution in understanding life. Landscape was part of this: most especially, the landscape of Cornwall. Through this wild place, it was surely possible to reach a more important understanding of human significance and of human insignificance. Through landscape we could appreciate where we had come from: the better to understand where we had to go. It was from Eden we had come: it was to Eden we should return. Or at least die in trying.

Does that sound frightfully adolescent? Well, so it bloody well should. We were bloody adolescents. Why do we sneer at adolescence? Why, when we look back in maturity at the wild notions and the demented hopes and the illogical beliefs and the ephemeral soul-deep passions of our adolescence, do we feel it our duty to sneer? Or apologise? Why do we not instead believe that adolescence is not a cursed but a blessed period of life: a white-water ride down the river of time. These rapids are not a place to spend a lifetime, but they are an essential transitional process if you wish to be an adult with any kind of life, any kind of passion, any kind of meaning. True, the stuff we came up with was half-baked: but then neither it nor we had been in the oven for terribly long. We were celebrating our newness, our rawness, celebrating the irrefragable fact that life was all before us: for us to change, for us to be changed irretrievably by.

So no: I don't have a single regret for all the bollocks we talked, for all the guff and blather that had so much meaning for us back then. Ralph and I would sit on the bouncy pile-carpet of thrift by Seagull Gully, looking down at the white birds wheeling in and out, or go down at Basher's Cove where the sea swept in with such style, or perhaps take our favourite spot at Bishop's Rock, a seat in an amphitheatre in which the stage was the sea. And we would talk of girls and love and God and society and life and death and books and landscape and painting and music and Joyce and Lawrence and girls: and all around us, the sea shifted and the landscape stayed still and things grew and things lived.

We were wild rebels: so obviously, we needed drugs to prove it to ourselves. Eventually, we managed to buy some. We got hold of some dope, or shit, as it then was called. We were staying in Cornwall, we had the cottage to ourselves (and if you don't leave it immaculate you will never go there again). We had left school by then, but we made a ceremonial return visit and, with splendid appropriateness, we arranged a deal in the tuck-shop. As a result, a package arrived at the cottage by post, humorously addressed to CC Kuper. It held an instruction: Do Not Burn. Generous of him to put that in: for this was grass, not shit, and we were hardly capable of telling them apart. It would have been a sad thing to set these expensive leaves on fire.

We had smoked before, but never really got off on it. Now, clumsily, with unpractised fingers, we skinned up a joint and daringly smoked it. We smoked until I noticed I was high. By the time this important fact had sunk in, I was, as we were to learn to say later, out of my head. I had to lie down for, it seemed, several weeks, half appalled and half delighted by the state I was in, half in terror and half in joy. Ralph, however, didn't smoke tobacco, and was unable to inhale the smoke. Instead, he swallowed it. While I was seeing visions and dreaming dreams, Ralph kept belching out great plumes of smoke – an alarming sight under the influence of mind-altering drugs – and complaining bitterly that it had no effect.

But a couple of weeks later, Ralph and I reconvened at Ted's house. We sat in his sunlit garden and smoked the rest of the stuff. Ralph had been practising hard with cigarettes, and had cracked the inhalation thing. Within a matter of moments he was out of his own head. I don't think I have ever seen anyone so sublimely happy: at the triumph of getting high, at the highness itself, at the garden, at what the garden revealed to him. The afternoon was, for all of us, a kind of ecstasy, the kind of ecstasy that unperplexes, but for Ralph, lying stretched out on the grass, it was a moment of ultimate perfection. After that, he was always keener on drugs than I was: mainly, as he has said many times, in a doomed attempt to refind that brief, but endlessly stretchy moment of joy. He kissed the earth, again and again: he could feel every blade of grass, he could feel the great movements of the entire planet shifting underneath him. He was at one with the earth. And he laughed.

It was, as we also learned to say, good stuff.

Drugs were part of life for a while. We dropped acid together: a great and fearful adventure. I hated it, to tell the truth, but because of the exigencies of the time, I had to pretend I loved it. In truth, my only good memory is the coming-down: a moment of soul-deep rejoicing in the fact that it was all beginning to be over. I seemed to be in a hammock in Ted's garden on another sun-filled day, transfixed by the beauties of a hoverfly. It hung in the air above me, motionless as time: a wild and beatific vision of everything that I loved.

Ralph and I were in Cornwall again. We had hitched down as usual. It was a beautiful day in May. Everything was perfect. Ralph decided to drop a trip; I declined his offer that I join him, though I pretended to think about it.

But Ralph was in sublime form, and I revelled in the contact-high of intimacy and acid. After a while we went for a walk along the cliff-tops: and we lay in a little hollow where the wind never penetrated. It was suddenly and astonishingly warm. Ralph stretched himself out to soak in the sun, to drink in the air, to embrace the landscape. And then a moment of high drama.

Ralph was on his feet, uttering a strange and fearful cry, one that chilled me as I turned to look at him: and there was a snake flying through the air: slim, slight, a couple of feet long, patterned unmistakably in black and white. "Christ! Oh Christ!"

"It's all right," I told him. "It was a grass snake. You were never in danger."

We sat for a while as Ralph thought this through. "You know, I wasn't frightened at all," he said eventually. "I only jumped up and shouted because I thought that was what you were supposed to do. I didn't really want it to go. I was rather disappointed. It felt beautiful. It crawled over my arm; I could feel it in such detail. It was... rather voluptuous, really." I didn't tell him it was an adder till the following day. Didn't want to upset him in his exalted state. Plenty of people drop acid and imagine that there are poisonous snakes crawling all over them: with Ralph the poisonous snakes were real. Talk about being at one with the earth.

Ralph went to live in the West Country. He has been a

teacher, worked on a sheep-ranch in Wyoming, he has done research on vernacular buildings, he has worked in recycling, he has completed a doctorate (*The Politics of Local Food*) and is currently working for the Devon Wildlife Trust. He has, in short, spent his life doing what he planned to do at school: working against the grain of society in order to make the world a better place. He was best man at my wedding, and is a friend to this day. I owe more to him than practically anyone else on the planet. We are united not only by our shared adolescence, but also by our love of the wild. This is something that we both learned over the course of years, but then I think we knew all along, even at the beginning, in Ted's garden and along the dizzy cliffs, that life wasn't really worth living without it.

6. Blackcap
Sylvia atricapilla

Room Six was the heart of it. Room Six had the view over the garden. Room Six was the place where we greeted the dawn and its songsters. Room Six was the place where the time that we wasted passed so very slowly. Ian Dury sang about the great trio – or should that be quartet? – of life's essentials, but looking back, I can see now that I never really cared for drugs or rock or roll. I just pretended to. I convinced myself that lying down on my back with a head full of Paki black listening to Emerson, Lake and Palmer was a meaningful experience. Remarkable what you can do when you put your – to use the term loosely – mind to it.

Room Six was in Burwalls. Burwalls Hall of Residence was in many ways an awful place. It was part of Bristol

University, but it pretended that it was part of Oxford University. It had formal dinners, occasions on which we were served unpleasant food while wearing academic gowns: no doubt a quintessential Oxfordian experience. Some of the girls who served the food were pretty, which was good, but someone said grace in Latin before we ate, which wasn't. It betrayed a too-flagrant wish that we were all in another place and were all other people.

But the Burwalls garden was a thing of wonder. It had mature trees and well-organised shrubs, formal beds, brutally pruned roses and a perfect lawn that rolled down from the main building in a series of steps, like agricultural terraces tilled through countless ages. It had an air of timeless devotion: as if gardens and the men to look after them were a prescriptive right of humankind. It was located just on the far side of Clifton Suspension Bridge; we crossed the bridge several times daily: we were on first-name terms with the wild gorge and its stern cliffs and with the River Avon far below. We had always before us the dramatic shape of the landscape: and we had a garden to walk through, gowned or ungowned as occasion dictated.

There were six of us in Room Six, at least to start with. Room Six was at the summit of the main building, which represented admirably the High Victorian Streaky Bacon School of Architecture. Room Six was tall, and had three lengthy sash windows, one of which led to a balcony on which three people could, with difficulty, stand. It was a good place to stand, because it overlooked the garden: the trees and shrubs falling away athletically.

Simon's really into nature, Brian told me, meaning not me but another. This Simon – sometimes referred to by Outsiders as Simon Heavy – was the lord of Room Six. "I wish I could get into nature like him," Brian said. And indeed, I had seen Simon, standing on the balcony of Room Six, favouring the garden with his solemn gaze, pale red hair about his shoulders and a Players Number Six in the hand that rested on the stone edge of the balcony. Gazing at nature: getting or being into it. To him was given the best room in the hall, to him was given the coolest room-mate, the aggressive, stocky, drug-gobbling Dave. Why was Simon Heavy in Room Six with Dave, while Simon Light was down in the Cottage annexe with an economist from Leicester called Mick? Life, it seemed, had its favourites. Why did Brian not take other people aside and tell them that Simon – no, not him, the other one, the one from the Garden annexe – was heavily into nature? And come to that, why wasn't I?

Simon and Dave actually lived in Room Six. They soon became accustomed to visits from the rest of us. We would troop up each evening after the unpleasant meal, and we talked and smoked cigarettes and listened to unpleasant records and drank instant coffee, shards of dried milk spinning on the surface of the liquid: me and Brian and

Jim and Tony in there with Dave and Simon. We smoked dope when we had any and established a dominance hierarchy, with one Simon at the top and the other on the bottom. Still, at least it was the right hierarchy. And the important thing to do was to smoke dope, which proved that we were superior to everyone else.

Strange to recall how important that was. It was not a matter of pleasure. It was a stern duty. We smoked to make the world a better place. We were all just about to rebuild the world with beauty and peace replacing aggression and ambition. Was that really such a terrible idea? Was it really so risible, to spend one's youth not looking to enjoy oneself but to try and improve the lot of humankind?

No doubt it was. All I can say was that it didn't seem so. Straight society was finished: the new society we were building was what mattered. Pass the joint, turn the LP over. Yes, what was it Joni said? We've got to get ourselves back to the garden. We all agreed with that. Growing up is supposed to be about the loss of innocence: our growing up was an attempt to find innocence. We believed that dope was the key; actually, at least for me, the key was as obvious as the garden all around us. Reaching keys is always a hard thing, as Alice had already shown me. Instead, we told each other that dope held the answers, and would suggest that what the Burwalls principal, or the housekeeper, or my tutor, or the president of the United States needed above all was a really good stiff joint. Then, presumably, they would see sense, declare peace, turn off their minds, relax and float downstream. This really wasn't the pursuit of pleasure: this stuff was the answer to every difficult thing the world had ever thrown up. The idea that everything – absolutely everything – was better when you were stoned was a core belief. When you were stoned, everything had a higher meaning: everything was more real: everything was more beautiful.

Simon failed to last the first term. He was kicked out of Burwalls after the cleaners discovered him enjoying a back-to-the-garden moment in Room Six with a girl called Miriam. Somehow, Tony and Dave managed to get themselves thrown out as well. By the time the second term began, Simon and Tony had a flat on the far side of Clifton, while Dave had joined a wild and anarchic establishment just the other side of the Suspension Bridge, a place I was to join myself a few months further on.

That left the rump of the Room Six Six marooned, leaderless and uncool in Burwalls. Brian was lightning swift, establishing a claim to Room Six and bringing Jim in with him. I was still, then, bottom of the hierarchy, but I was morally a part of that room. Each evening as supper ended we repaired to its heights. I would sit cross-legged on one or other of the beds, an album sleeve across my lap, and commence the ritual magic of the Rizlas and the shredded Number Six and the rolled cardboard and, of course, the hash itself. We were seeking something: but

also, Jim and I were perhaps trying to recapture something.

Jim and I had shared a night in Room Six with Dave
and Tony in the first couple of weeks. Dave and Tony
were "doing acid", which was far beyond my ambitions at
the time; Jim and I were there as supporters, disc jockeys,
joint-rollers, good-vibes bringers. At a certain stage, it was
decided that since it was so late, the only thing to do was
to stay up and see the dawn. This was, of course, a Cosmic
Experience. That's what the times were about: a search for
experiences with meaning and beauty, moments about
which there was a touch of eternity. Jim and I would
sometimes smoke a joint on the Suspension Bridge, gazing
at the gorge's immensities... failing to understand that for
me, at least, the answers, and for that matter, all the interesting questions, were to be found, not in the confusions
of the drug but in the certainties of the gorge and the wildness of nature all around it. I see now that I was entirely
taken up with the wrong kind of grass. And so, joint
smoked, we would drop the roach over the edge and watch
it tumble down and down and down, red ember winking at
us as it fell, like the indicator on a car's headlights. No left
turn unstoned, we said to each other, and giggled.

That's the only thing I miss about dope-smoking. Ah,
the helpless laughter, the real, unending, weeping laughter, all dignity gone, when you beg for it to stop because
your belly aches so, and you and your companions are

united by something beyond mere hilarity. Was it the laughter of Mozart that we read about in *Steppenwolf*? Was it the laughter of the spheres? Jim once said: "I know some very noisy sheep," and we laughed for a couple of hours. Could anything be better, be richer than that? And was this laughter the gift of dope, or the gift of youth? Either way, I will never know it again: times when it seemed that God was in his heaven and smoking joints alongside us. All on the same side. And all into nature.

Dawn duly came, as we thought it might, but it was a miracle nonetheless. We looked out across the October garden and the lemon sun gave it a light. Dave retreated from the balcony to put "Here Comes the Sun" on the stereo and we smoked a joint, the last, contemplating the miracle, and if there were tears in Jim's eyes, no doubt there were in mine. The plants of the garden – the garden we had to get back to – were growing before us, while the smoke of burning botanic substances – our proposed route to this garden – was in our lungs, and its virtues or its vices were fizzing in our heads. We were young and foolish and still growing as the garden grew before us.

Jim and Brian and I attempted to keep the Room Six thing going. We weren't as cool as the departed trio, but we did our best. Me, I felt that Jim rather let the side down in the matter of Rudi's dope. Rudi had got The Fear and lent Jim a biggish lump of dope so that the Pigs wouldn't get him. We were smoking our way through this very acceptable loan when Jim saw a Pig in the very corridors of Burwalls. Jim at once got The Fear himself, and ran up the stairs three at a time to Room Six, where Brian and I were enjoying yet another sampling of Rudi's dope. Jim seized the plastic bag that contained it, opened the window and whirled the bag around his head like the young David with his sling. In this manner, he hurled five quids' worth of perfectly decent Moroccan into the trees. Brian and I failed to find it despite a lengthy search. It turned out that the Pig in question was there to investigate the question of a stolen bicycle.

But I was soon off exploring thrilling possibilities beyond Burwalls: penetrating into Clifton, visiting Simon, Dave and Tony, and meeting thrilling girls: Miriam, and especially her best friend Lesley. Brian met a darkly pretty girl called Janet, and was at once utterly taken up. But all the same, there was some sort of default mechanism in place, one that threw the three of us together in Room Six on a regular basis.

Getting into nature. Sometimes, that meant nothing more than listening to Pink Floyd in a darkened smoke-filled room. The Incredible String Band pleased me far more: I still maintain that the sitar is an underrated rock instrument. In some ways, cultivating a love of nature was a search for maturity, for no one is less aware of the wild world around him than a teenager, who would turn down an hour at the most beautiful place on the planet for ten minutes in the bus shelter with his mates. In another way, we were striving for something beyond the ordinary, beyond the obvious: for the world undiscovered by Straight Society. And, in a curious way, there was a time when everything in Room Six was perfect, when we seemed to have found what we were looking for. Or at least, to be on the brink of finding it.

In my memory this enchanted period lasted an entire summer, but that can't be right. Perhaps it was just a few days, between the exams and the long, long vacation. It seemed to stretch on, though, for night after night: a series of ancient revels, sacred rites as spring turned to summer, and we three were up there in Room Six stoned again (we had acquired some of the light, almost champagne-like grass full of cheerfully exploding seeds), the stereo (Brian's, 30 quid from Boots) doing its stuff and the talk and the noise-filled silence and the laughter. And with it, the sense, ridiculously futile but utterly compelling, that we were on our way to reaching something beyond ourselves: that we were part of a great global phenomenon, a move towards a better way to live, and a better way of understanding the world. And time and again we would open the curtains and peer though the smoke at the spreading light, and then raise the giant sash windows and bring in the deafening sound of song: "Oh God! It's the fucking tweeties again!" We compared the din unfavourably with Captain Beefheart playing the sax, but we stood on the balcony and listened to it anyway and hid the roaches away from prying eyes when all was done.

It was the garden that made these times idyllic, or at least it seemed to have done so in my memory: the lovingly mown sward, or series of swards, the grand trees, their inseparable songsters. What were they? It seems astonishing that I couldn't pick out a single one of them in those days. Today, drunk or sober, I could name every bird that sang there. What would we have been listening to? Well, blue tit and great tit and chaffinch and wren and robin and dunnock and blackbird and song thrush; that's for certain, along with house sparrow and wood pigeon and greenfinch. Maybe a crow or two. Nuthatch, I'll bet, and mistle thrush. Woodpeckers, green and great spotted, certainly, and maybe lesser as well. And the migrant warblers: there'd surely have been chiffchaffs and garden warblers. And certainly there'd have been blackcap: that rich, bubbling song, fruity and fluty, a great favourite of mine. But in those days all I heard was the music of the spheres, or the soundtrack of the cosmos, and if it was good, it wasn't enough. I needed more precision: perhaps we all did. But at the time, a love, unspecific and directed in the manner of a scatter-gun, seemed enough.

The garden was a lovely thing, and indeed, I dallied there briefly with one of the waitresses who served us at our formal meals: but this was an informal occasion and we were ungowned. When I left Burwalls at the end of the summer term, I borrowed a wheelbarrow from the gardener, along with the extension that made the thing twice as deep, which he used when collecting autumnal sweepings. I put my books and my clothes into this capacious vehicle and trundled it across the Suspension Bridge to West Mall, to Dave's flat, and moved in. Ready for some new adventures. It struck me that I had more to learn about nature.

Jim stopped smoking dope that summer; I rather think Brian did the same, though we lost touch. I took less and less pleasure in the late-night sessions and stopped smoking the stuff entirely a year or so later. Simon, the cool one, the one that wasn't me, became a writer and a traveller and, it must be said, a great adventurer and lover, and worked for National Geographic. We are still friends. Jim makes films for television and wrote a book about Abelard and Heloise and is working on another about Dante; we also remain friends and he is godfather to my older boy. Brian became a solicitor and married Janet, which was a wise thing to do. Dave and Tony, alas, were undone by that ruinous stuff LSD, a desperate waste of two fine people.

7. Red deer
Cervus elephus

For a while, I was a creature of the night: a moth, a bat (a greater horseshoe bat, of course), an aye-aye. Night-walking answered a profound need: a vast suite of needs. When the fit was on me, I would set off into the black, marching rather than strolling, always with the wild gorge as the centre-point and about one a.m. as the average starting-time. This walking was essential for many reasons. For a start, I lived in a madhouse. My flat comprised two gloriously elegant and unspeakably sordid rooms on the drawing-room floor of a house in Clifton, dramatic, peeling and austere. To be more pedantic, the flat was one enormous room divided by folding doors and a kind of proscenium arch. It was utterly lovely, decaying, crumbling, filled with a random collection of tenants, and intermittently full of strangers. It housed, albeit intermittently, three other rent-payers, at least at the beginning, paying £2 a week each. You never knew how many people you would find behind the door when you opened it: sometimes many, sometimes none, sometimes a couple in search of solitude, sometimes several, sometimes a large gathering of hard-smoking truth-seekers, sometimes a crowd of strangers, sometimes a cluster of lovely women. I was something of an eccentric: I occasionally cleaned things, washed things up, cooked. (Oddly enough, one of our number became a rather talented chef.) The flat in the film *Withnail and I* was not dissimilar in general principles, but in the film they toned it down, in order to make it believable.

From this flat in its gracious and tree-lined square – mad old woman on the ground floor, jazz band in the basement – I would set out, sometimes in search of company, sometimes in search of solitude. Sometimes I was just in search of violent movement, for I could never bear to be cooped up for long. But above all, I was seeking some kind of order, some kind of calm, some way of achieving an understanding of the night. Many things drove me to these mad marches: mostly madness itself, for on the whole it was sanity I was seeking. At times I made these walks in company, to talk about great things, or just to walk, and then sit on a bench and smoke a cigarette, moments at which it seemed that the entire universe was back under control, no longer spinning off its axis in that disconcerting way that universes have when you are young.

Sometimes these nocturnal jaunts were taken when drug-addled. On these occasions, when I was in company, we would often climb over the wall into Ashton Park, gates locked at sunset, and walk the wooded paths in fatuous wonder. But more often, I would take to the streets alone: to clear my mind on those evenings when smoke-filled rooms and ditto minds became intolerable: when the thought of listening to one more rock album in the company of the same horizontal figures – upright only to roll another one – was more than I could bear. I would set off on another march and the cool air would wash my forehead and my temples and the rhythm of marching would still my thoughts and calm my anxieties and the night would show me that there was, indeed, more to the universe than four walls, Jerry Garcia and Paki black. The all-male nature of such gatherings also oppressed me: I wanted to find female company instead; no doubt when I did so, Mrs Watson would have rebuked me for this weakness and told me: "Go and take drugs with the boys!"

Other matters also took me to the streets, and out to the downs, the woods and the wilds. And sometimes, rather often in fact, it was something to do with writing. I didn't walk to seek inspiration, though. Mostly, I walked because there was none to be had. I knew, in some strange way, that I was a writer. The only problem with this little chunk of self-realisation was that I didn't actually write anything. Not much, anyway: little passages and patches, bad prose and worse poems, and nothing that ever added up, nothing that ever came remotely close to saying anything about anything that mattered. "It's just a question of being honest," people told me, when talking about their own attempts to write. I wondered if that was the problem: if what I lacked was not talent but honesty.

But then I wondered, feet marching in sudden proud rhythm like Stephen Dedalus, what has honesty to do with writing? If honesty was all it took be a writer, then everyone in Bristol might as well be a writer. I knew, as I walked the streets, that honesty wasn't the answer. It was words. But what did I want them to say? What order did I want to put them in? How did anyone ever finish anything? All those doodles and snatches and verses and paragraphs: did they mean that I was a writer? Or did their lack of completion mean that I was nothing of the kind? And for that matter, why did nobody think my stuff was any good?

Most often of all, though, it was girls that drove me out into the night. Not physically, not normally, anyway. Just thinking about girls was enough: if I thought about girls for too long, I'd have to be out there again, walking across the Suspension Bridge and looping back down to the river, or crossing the river at the lock gate and climbing to the downs. Often I would take the wild hairpinning path that led to the foot of the gorge, sometimes going down that way, at other times using it to make a breathless ascent. Sometimes, normally when in company, I would visit the Venturers, the all-night café, drink pints of tea, eat bacon sandwiches and observe the clientele of sleepy drivers and preternaturally wakeful drug-users. Sometimes police cars stopped me on my walks, for such activities, though not illegal, were unseemly to the policemanly mind. I would answer their questions politely enough, and then walk on, up the endless hills of Clifton and down the sweeping descents.

Invariably, the act of walking, the exposure to places a little wilder than the floor of my flat or the floor of other people's flats, than the bed in my flat or the beds in others people's flats, would calm my mind. Walking is not an aid to thought: it is an aid to thoughtlessness. It is as near as the Western world gets to meditation: walking brings a mindlessness which can soothe in times of trouble, and into which important matters sometimes leap all unexpected.

But I was talking about girls. I remember a line about love from somewhere: "Today was happy until luncheon". All the anxieties of a bad yet necessary love seem caught up in these few words: the anxiety when things are going badly, the still greater anxiety when things are going well. Sometimes love seems to have nothing whatsoever to do with joy: it is a state of uninterrupted worry, a constant sense of needling nagging failure, a feeling of never being quite up to the demands imposed, an ache in which physical desire seems to play almost no part at all. At other times, you find yourself involved for no reason that you can explain to yourself: a love affair that seems to have been embarked on solely out of a desire to pursue one's education, to find out what you are like and what women are like. It is customary to try and paint the picture of the love life of one's youth as one long round of orgiastic excess. For the most part, so far as I remember, such set-pieces played a relatively minor role. More often, love was a matter of exploration and confusion, error and counter-error, every manoeuvre made more complex by the lack of any notion whatsoever about what life is all about and what either of us or any of us wanted to do in it.

Ashton Court lies on the far side of the Clifton Suspension Bridge: just walk past Burwalls and keep going. It was a splendid, dramatically undulating piece of parkland, of the kind I was later to find mirrored in the African savannah: open grass punctuated by imposing trees, their lower branches and leaves trimmed in a straight line by the creatures that inhabited the place. A browse-line, it is called: and different creatures produce the same effect in different places. In Africa, it's antelope. And Ashton Court, with its different browsing creatures, was not without a certain magic. The shadowy beauties of the landscape were fine and impressive: and it was an incomparable joy to have these big spaces, these giant trees, for my own. It was a personal Eden, but I never had any thoughts of playing Adam and Eve there. Did I suggest this walk, this desperate venture, late one evening? Or did she? Either way, it was the spiritual possibilities of the place that drew us there, and it was the spiritual ones that sustained us when we arrived. We crossed the Suspension Bridge, the lights of the town below us, the river far beneath. We were unstoned. We passed Burwalls: I could see the balcony of Room Six, from which one could greet the dawn. We reached the place I knew well, where the wall dipped and there was a foothold. She was wearing a skirt that swept the ground, but then she always did: she whisked it back to the thighs to climb in. She looked lovely; I said nothing, nor did she. We were just there for a walk in the moonlight. I had no hopes, no plans. It was perhaps one in the morning.

There was always a delicious wickedness about walking in Ashton Court in these forbidden times of darkness. I remember the big sward, our two moon-shadows marching before us: the trees standing huge, but miraculously drained of all colour, as is the strange way of moonlight. Perhaps we held hands: but if so, it was only because of the beauties of the place.

And something happened. Something very beautiful and very mysterious. We walked into a herd of deer. We could see them, not well, in the moonlight: dark shapes picked out by the easily visible pallor beneath their tails.

This is the caudal patch, I can now tell you, and I now know that its purpose is to flash a warning about danger – they turn their backs on the source of danger, raise their tails, expose their white bums and leg it – should it be the moment to run away. But miraculously, it wasn't. Perhaps it should have been. But we stayed quiet and still: so did they: us incredulous, them nervous. Their enormous size, their colossal numbers: we seemed in some strange way to be in danger ourselves. We were, though not from the deer. I'm certain we held hands then. Do I imagine the click of the antlers? Have I superimposed such observations, from many subsequent African experiences of great proximity to wildlife, over what happened that night? Certainly I remember the way they looked at us: over their shoulders, solemn-eyed, big-eared. I remember hinds and stags together, though that may not be right. The main impression was of numbers: of huge and shadowed forms: of a profound and utterly different way of living and seeing and understanding the world. It was like an alien landing: creatures that seemed far from us: yet creatures we had some kind of important link with. They seemed wholly real, unnaturally so: yet also they seemed like a fiction, as if we had imagined them, somehow summoned them up by the power of a shared fantasy, as if we had, indeed, got ourselves back to the garden. Very softly, we crept away. Their power was all on us now: the power of place, the power of the wild world. We seemed scarcely human: never more human.

At the top of a long rise, we stopped to rest, looking out over the perfect sculpted land that fell away. We found that we were in the fork of an immense fallen tree: cosy, hidden between the splayed thighs of its commodious branches, in the great woody crotch of the tumbled giantess. So we kissed. How could we not? We did more, not for pleasure but out of a sense of duty to this wild spot, to the wild creatures we had encountered. The power of the place, the power of the wild world had called us. We were beyond the reach of the tame world now.

8. Water vole
Arvicola terrestris

There is a terrible danger when you make a transition from one element to another. If you get it wrong, you get the bends. If you make the transition in the wrong way, or too fast, or with too much confidence, you can find yourself in trouble. And it looked to me the most terrible step anybody could be asked to take: to move into grown-up life.

Was it harder to make that step, back in those days? To suppose that life was harder for us than it is for subsequent generations is, after all, the inalienable right of every mature human. I don't suppose it really was, but all the same, the fact is that we were not simply making a simple change from feckless studenthood to the inevitable horrors of earning a living. Today's feckless students are all well aware that real life is ultimately unavoidable. But we really believed that we would be able to fly by those nets. When we joined the grown-up world, we had to accept something that none of us thought could ever happen. We had to come to terms with an about-face in reality. We had to acknowledge an error in the way we saw the world. We had to accept failure: for hadn't we all vowed that we would never return to straight society, that we would for ever live our lives by some sort of code that lay between Hermann Hesse and the Grateful Dead? I was caught between certainties. And, still groping for the meaning and understanding that I would have when I was on proper neighbourly terms with the wild world, I seemed to be cut adrift. Words I had howled a million times on stoned nights, words I had sometimes hummed boastfully to myself on solitary walks, words I had taken to myself as a proud affectation, now became uncomfortably packed with relevance. No direction home.

These days I write for *The Times*, about sport as well as wildlife. Some of the letters I have received from readers over the years: well, they make me wonder. I mean, the letters from earnest young people all wanting to take up a job in sports journalism, just as I have. What should I do? they ask. How should I prepare for this great step? Youth for them seems to be nothing more than a preparation for a career: education merely a necessary step towards the attainment of a high salary. They send me their terrifying

CVs. They ask me what university course they should take. Should they read journalism? (God no, journalism is for doing, not studying, and besides, do you want to spend three years reading me, or Shakespeare? Work it out for yourself. You should educate yourself for the sake of education, not for the sake of a job.)

Me, educated, at least up to a point, for the sake of education alone, well, I had a plan. I was not going to rejoin straight society. I was going to take on some salt-of-the-earth dignity-of-labour sort of job and write great works in my spare time. At various times, I worked in a butter factory, as a navvy, and in a cake factory, for strange as it seems, it was easy to get low-grade work in those days. Alas, I swiftly made the discovery that if you take on a full-time manual job, you are too knackered to write anything when you get home. It was also becoming obvious that I couldn't do anything with any competence except write.

So I went on the dole and wrote. I began to keep office hours, amazing myself and my visitors by repelling them until the hour of six. I started trying to write for money. At the same time, I began looking for full-time jobs in journalism. Having made this epic decision to rejoin straight society, I had a terrible shock. Straight society was no more keen on being joined than I was on joining it. It took months. I thought it would never happen, but in the end, I got an interview for a job on the *Surrey Mirror*. I dressed with horror and care, in a suit unworn since my interview for university, and a tie, a garment I had vowed would never again hang from my neck. Once there, I explained why I had always wanted to be a journalist. I remembered not to say "because I can't think of anything else". "What is your fantasy of yourself as a journalist?" I was asked, as if this were a question of remarkable brilliance. I said I wanted to be a war correspondent: it seemed the sort of answer that would please. I got the job: a vista of horrors opened before me.

In all this, I was supported and encouraged by Ruth. Ruth, tall and kind and lovely. She was going to stick by me. She was going to be a teacher: after a series of great adventures and tremendous travels, she too had decided that straight society was beckoning. The *Surrey Mirror* told me to start in July; Ruth then managed to get a place in a teacher training college in Streatham, of all places. I made a second trip to Surrey and managed to rent a room in a house. In this manner, we were launched together onto a grown-up world that didn't really want us. We arrived at the house: I started work the following day. My life sentence was about to begin. I seemed to have nothing left but Ruth: well, I reasoned, and rightly, that was a hell of a lot more than most people in straight society.

The house was in a place called Hookwood. Hookwood is hard by Gatwick Airport. We were living, not with a gang of hippy students with *Journey to the East* and

Bhagavad Gita on their shelves, but with a builder called Derek. Derek had a girlfriend, whom he entertained in the evening, and a secretary who served him in the morning. This led to loud public arguments. There was also a madwoman. She ran a cattery from her home but no longer lived there because, as she explained helpfully, her husband was plotting to murder her. We were a merry household.

Work was pretty bad for me, but it was worse for Ruth. She got a job making airline meals. Still, at least she knew she would be stopping it in October, when term began. This was what I would be doing for the rest of my life. I had – the horror! The horror! – to deal with suits and ties and endless conversations about cars. A personal means of transport was a prerequisite for the job: I bought an 80cc motorbike which I loathed and feared. On this horrible contraption I got out around Redhill and Reigate to make futile efforts at fact-gathering and returned to the office to try and write it all up as news stories.

I thought I could write: I found I could do nothing of the kind. I thought I was smart: I discovered I was an idiot. The simple craft of writing a news story for a local paper was set about with insuperable difficulties. I never seemed to establish a fact, never seemed to make a contact. I still had long hair: that didn't help. I struggled: for a while it seemed that I might suffer the ultimate ignominy and fail to make it, sacked during the trial period, unable to do my indentures, thrown out of the profession of journalism, and no doubt every other profession as well. My colleagues were not even remotely like my friends from university. I had to accept that some of them voted Conservative, had no sympathy with any progressive movement, wanted only a nicer car and a better job. I had thought such people were the fantasies of overwrought student minds.

Back "home", things were not much more amusing. Ruth would be exhausted from a day on her feet putting together "meals"; I would be bewildered and stressed. We would cook food in the shared kitchen, sometimes watch television, while the madwoman harangued us disjointedly. Derek lurked in his room, from which raised voices or the sounds of reconciliation could frequently be heard. Sometimes the madwoman played the radio at full volume while we watched television, in order to assert some important point of communal living.

And so we went to the pub. True, this was something of an extravagance, but since our sanity was involved, it was money well spent. The pub was a 15-minute walk away and it was called, unpromisingly, Ye Olde Six Bells. It was a hot summer: the pub had a garden. It was always full of Gatwick types: adulterous pilots luring willing hosties to their doom and so forth. There being many such people, the place was always crowded to an almost ludicrous degree. There was never a chair to sit on, inside or out. So we established a routine: Ruth would find a patch of grass to sit on, as near to the river as possible, and I would brave the pub itself. It would take about 15 minutes to get served, so I adopted a policy of buying two drinks at once, or rather four, and then carrying them out to see what sort of vantage point Ruth had secured for us.

It was, astonishingly enough, a rather lovely place. The River Mole flowed past and the garden reached the river's edge. And it was here that I, that we, found respite from the insoluble problems of weaselling our way into the grown-up world. Watching the river go past is one of life's most riveting occupations: the thinking man's television – and it is all the more soothing after a day trying to be a grown-up, telephoning Reigate and Banstead Borough Council and asking, must someone be killed before something is done about the Buckland bends? Planning applications, rows about council houses, knocking on doors – would you say it was hell living here? – failing to whip up non-controversies, trying to remember to get the big facts in the intro, remembering when to say "alleged", finding that that bastard Coulson was unavailable for comment as usual, writing something about traffic lights, writing something about dogshit ("walking along this path is like playing hopscotch"), looking for the local angle, doing stuff about parking, interviewing friends of the editor from the Rotary Club, and occasionally, as a real treat, doing a story about pets. A year before I had been trying to write stuff that would take in the entire sweep of the cosmos: now I was restricted to Redhill: with, it must be said, Reigate, not to mention Merstham, Salfords, Earlswood, Bletchingly and Betchworth – though not, of course, Caterham, Godstone or Oxted. That would be going too far.

Having my work despised by people I despised. Learning not to despise the people I despised. Learning, humiliatingly, that the people I despised could do – and write – some things infinitely better than I could. Realising that such talents as I possessed were not terribly helpful to the profession of hard news journalism. Knowing that there was nothing else I could conceivably do. But never mind: at least, every two or three days, when I didn't have a night job, Ruth and I could go to the pub: I could drink my two pints of beer, and we could then walk home with my arm about her waist, for, tall and slim and elegant as she was, I couldn't reach her shoulder with any degree of comfort. There was nothing, then, to complain of.

It was even better than I have let on, that place by the river. Most evenings, as we sat and watched it doing its stuff, we would see a small bow-wave move urgently from one side to the other. Sometimes back again. It had a brown little face with whiskers. A grave, round face, with the same twinkle in its eyes... Small neat ears and thick silky hair. It was the water rat!... Lines from *The Wind in the Willows*, a book I had adored, read, reread, and even rewritten, in riverbank tales of my own.

I loved Ratty best of all, though I had never, till I came to Hookwood, seen a real one. And even without literary and personal associations, the water vole, to give him his proper name, is the most winning of creatures: a little, furry, wet-loving teddy, pursuing its life with great seriousness right in front of us. It was the pub, the river, the beer, the water-vole that made everything all right. It really was. The water vole put a little magic into daily life: he gave us a small reward for the huge efforts we were making to become grown-up. Because of the water vole, we found ourselves able to function in this alien and grown-up world.

Drinking with Ratty told us that we needn't grow up altogether: that small things could still give delight: that the world had its solace even for people who prepared airline food, even for people who had ridden the hateful little motorbike all the way to Bletchingly and back and still failed to get the story.

The Hookwood water vole was our passport into the adult world: a furry specific against the bends. We hadn't entirely left the world of wonders behind. Even though we were marooned in a commuter village and trapped in jobs that offered little satisfaction and surrounded by alien and unsympathetic beings, there was delight to be found in the world. We had a pub, we had a river, we had pints, we had a vole: and we were together. As a result, we made it. By the time the autumn had come, we had a flat in south London with a troop of friends, Ruth started her course and enjoyed it, and I began to find some kind of accommodation with the demands of news-gathering. Hookwood had put us to what seemed a pretty extreme test: and yet we passed. Ruth got us through: for that, eternal thanks. She did it, with the help of the water voles.

9. Himalayan pied kingfisher
Ceryle lugubris

For a time, we were four. It is a period that many people go through at a certain time in life: paired off but not yet procreating, bravely independent yet still seeking some kind of familial closeness. It is, I suppose, a relatively new kind of relationship, an aspect of contraception and the end of the extended family. And there we were: me and Ruth and Mark and Lucy. I suppose we spent three or four evenings a week in each other's company.

Lucy and I met as colleagues on the *Surrey Mirror*. She was small and pretty, thrillingly strong-minded and being Indian, gorgeously brown of skin. Naturally, I made a pass at her at the Christmas party, for no journalist can resist a cliché. She explained that she had a boyfriend to go home to: the fact that I had Ruth to go home to had momentarily escaped my attention. After that, Lucy and I became friends instead. So then we met each other's partners, and we all four became friends: each individual relationship drawing strength from, almost defined by the others.

I worked it out graphically: a square with a person at each corner, each linked either by the side of a square or a diagonal. That makes six lines, six relationships in all. Or should that be 12? Do you count, say, my relationship with Lucy as one relationship or as two, to include her relationship with me? You decide.

If I were writing about these six or 12 relationships in a novel, I would naturally bring in all kinds of subtle sexual interplay between the four characters. It would be against nature if this were not the case. Desire, conscious or not, would add a thrilling subtext to the easy, ostensibly innocent times we spent together. Surely we would seek for little moments when we could be alone with the wrong partner, the whiff of the swap never entirely absent, the tiny seeds of jealousy implanted when one opposed pair seemed to be having too good a time together. The diagonals are the thrilling ones for a novelist: the line that linked me and Lucy and the one that linked Ruth and Mark. It was inevitable that there would be sexual tensions: such things are a staple of human life: you can see it all in *A Midsummer Night's Dream*, after they had taken a love-potion; it was there in the BBC series, *The Good Life*, after they had overdone the pea-pod burgundy, clearly another love potion.

But it really wasn't like that with me and Lucy, despite the pass and the miss. Oh, I never minded looking at her, never avoided the chance to throw the occasional discreet glance in the direction of her trim body as she dressed or undressed, at times when we found ourselves sharing accommodation. But there never was a flirtatious thing between us. Nor was she the sister I never had: I have two perfectly good sisters of my own. If anything, she was the brother I never had: teasing, competitive, sporty, bantering.

I was prepared to have a sticky relationship with Mark. I thought he would resent my admiration for Lucy, suspect the purity of my motives in befriending her, and that we would establish a relationship based on polite male head-butting. But not a bit of it. We established the great anti-thetical friendship of my life: sometimes I think we have nothing in common except our friendship. He trained as an engineer, moved seamlessly into the world of computers, was always effective at making money while being well aware that other things in life mattered more. He was immensely practical and could do absolutely anything. I was fascinated by his ability to fix things. He used to fix cars and motorbikes as a matter of course, but nothing stayed broken around him for long. I was enthralled by the way he fixed his digital watch: how can anybody do that?

He played the guitar, hated folk music with a strange passion, had little interest in sport unless he was doing it himself. He liked to have loud music playing around him most of the time: I love Bach, birdsong and quiet. And yet, by the magical process in which friendships happen, Mark and I were friends at once.

Ruth and Lucy established a friendship just as quickly. Ruth was naturally concerned when she first heard my tactless accounts of Lucy's qualities, but Lucy's nature made it immediately clear that there was no flirtation involved. And as for the other diagonal, the Mark–Ruth line, that, so far as I know, had no elements at all of thwarted desire. Rather they had an easy brother–sister relationship that completed the four-sided nature of our friendship.

We mostly expressed this by going into the pub together: often the Tulse Hill Tavern. There was a garden, where we sat when the weather permitted. We all had the same drink, which simplified matters: perhaps there was a sound bit of feminism in action here; no pints for the boys and halves for the ladies. We drank the drink that was then called Pils: a pilsner made by Holsten that was then rather in vogue, a forerunner of the designer lagers and foreign bottled beers that became so fashionable later. Lord knows what we talked about or what we laughed about. It doesn't really matter. Whatever we did, it was a shared celebration of the fact that we were all in the grown-up world and surviving: and what's more, we were doing so while retaining many of the things in our youth that we still treasured: things like laughter, frivolity, talk, friendship.

And then came the drink at the Tulse Hill Tavern that changed everything, that made the four-cornered friendship, for a while, the central matter of our lives. I had made a rather decent bit of money with some freelance work, and I was wondering how best to get rid of it. My plan was to spend some of it on a stereo and some of it on a mildly exciting bit of travel. I asked Lucy's advice, for she was (and indeed is) a great travel bore. At the time, she was planning a trip back to India, to see her father and to see a bit of the country with Mark.

Now one of the things about strict sexual equality in drinking is that women have smaller livers than men. As a result, women can't process alcohol as efficiently as men. To put it bluntly, all things being equal, if they drink on equal terms they get pissed quicker. This was always disputed by Lucy, but then most things were. "It simply has no effect on me!"

Anyway, the evening was a good one, and we kept going back for another four bottles of Pils, and we were loud and hilarious and happy. Eventually, and perhaps inevitably, Lucy, no doubt affected by the smallness of her liver, said: "Bollocks to your stereo. Spend it all on travel! Come to India with us!" That was nice and friendly and utterly impractical, because she was leaving in a fortnight.

I said these things: but Lucy was unstoppable. This should not have surprised me: unstoppability is perhaps her defining trait, and perhaps doubly so when inflamed by the Pils. She argued and bullied us: for she was now set on the idea of bringing us to India. As more and then more Pils were purchased, so the inevitability of the journey made itself plain. By the time we left the pub, we were committed.

I had never seen myself as the sort of person who went out of Europe. I had thought I was a safe-options sort of chap. But I found myself on a plane and bound for Delhi: and then living the strange dream of arrival. It began with heat, 50 degrees of it, and jet lag, a new experience, and culture shock that deprived me of speech for several days. I remember lying on a bed in the YMCA on that first morning sweating and listening to the sounds of two maniacs playing tennis. It was doubly hot because Ruth refused to have the ceiling fan on: she was afraid it would come loose and go spinning about the room in a generally decapitatory fashion. It was of course Lucy who made the decision to leave that very night: and so we took the train to Jammu. The following morning, mad with sleep deprivation, we entered a scrum and somehow emerged with four tickets for the bus. After that, the eight-hour journey into the hills: the ever steeper, ever more dramatic hills of Kashmir, and a notice that read: "This is not a race or a rally! Drive slow and enjoy Kashmir Valley!" Valleys and hills: hills becoming mountains, mountains becoming the most stirring peaks on earth: before us, impossibly but incontrovertibly, the vertical white walls of the Himalaya.

We hired a houseboat on Dal Lake in Srinagar. We walked the streets, we travelled the waterways by *shikara*, poled about in these crafts of sybaritic luxury. I fell in love with a thousand women, all veiled in the same stunning shade of blue: a kingfisher colour that often went with darkly flirtatious eyes. Every detail of the place was an enchantment. Time and again, I found myself looking at the vignettes of Kashmiri life and wondering at the miracle that I was in the same place: I am in this street with this person, I am standing here looking at that mountain, I am being propelled across the water by this glorious woman. The priorities of the world were remade.

There was a kingfisher that fished from the slim wires that connected our craft to the shore. It was confirmation, if confirmation were needed, that we were living in a land of magic. It provided a wonderful cabaret, totally unafraid, giving a blowtorch stare at the water and occasionally launching itself in. Mark, fascinated, characteristically started to calculate the success rate: the figure eludes me, but the bird's efficiency was as stunning as its colours.

We made many long excursions through the lakes, riding the *shikaras*, lying back on the cushions that made a gigantic double bed on which we lay haphazardly, mildly intertwined, gazing at the passing parade of beauty and wonder. There is still a photograph from that time, taken by a boatman, the girls lovely, one brown, the other browner, Mark and I, utterly content in our closed society of four. It was a time of almost religious enlightenment: as if this friendship, this shared pilgrimage into grown-up life, was made all right, was made safe, was even made good by the fact that we could, all four of us together, ride the waters of Dal Lake and inspect kingfishers.

And there was a second kingfisher. This one was much more seldom seen. It was huge, nearly the size of a crow, and black and white: but it was unmistakably a kingfisher, a sword-billed starer at the water, a plunger, a seizer and a swallower. It liked darker, more sheltered places, and, obviously, bigger fish. It was a different species because it lived in a different way: a revelation not only of biodiversity, but also of the reason for biodiversity. Each bird inhabited a different ecological niche: and I had not thought the world possessed a multiplicity of kingfishers. These days, I have on my shelves an ornithological monograph on the most outrageously colourful birds you could possibly set eyes on: *Kingfishers, Bee-eaters and Rollers*. It lists 87 species of kingfisher, and doesn't include the Himalayan pied, which it considers a subspecies of pied kingfisher; the scientific name in the title of this chapter comes from another authority. My experience on Dal Lake makes me want to believe that despite the monograph, the Himalayan pied is a good species. But I knew nothing of taxonomy then, still less its changing (like bottled beer) fashions. I knew only the sensational fact that there were two different kinds of kingfisher, and that was a joy enough.

New possibilities opened before me. I thought they were all to do with travel and friendship and personal development: and I was wrong. It was just that the power of four had brought me to this place, this realisation: a small adventure that inevitably led to much greater ones. I was scarcely aware of it, with all the distractions and delights and excitements of that journey, but the more muted, the more subtle sense of wonder at this, the second kind of kingfisher, had struck extraordinarily deep. I was still not fully awakened, but I was aware of my wonder, my delight in this strange vision of the Other Kingfisher. I had a vague idea of what it meant. I felt some kind of summons in this vision, a need to know more, understand more, see more.

I half misunderstood it, but only half. Certainly, as soon as I returned to England, I resolved to go and live in Asia. I was changed: I was a traveller, I was a chancer, I was an adventurer. I wanted to seek strange things and see strange sights and listen to strange sounds and breathe strange air. I still didn't know what I wanted to seek: but at least I had got as far as knowing that I was a seeker.

10. Huntsman spider
Heteropoda venatoria

The flat was perfect. It had one large, generous room, five-sided, its two outer walls meeting at a shallow angle. There was also a small bedroom, smaller bathroom, imperceptible kitchen. It was on the 15th floor. The big windows looked down on the amazing cityscape spread out beneath: between the high-rises, as if through forest trees, the harbour danced before us. Hong Kong means Fragrant Harbour. We could see the fussy ferries stolidly performing their tasks, the rotund sampans doing whatever sampans do, big ships, liners, container ships, disreputable Conradian cargo vessels, junks, high and square-ended like Spanish galleons, every now and then, one of them sprouting a batwing sail. We were at the bottom of the Mid-Levels, a bit on the respectable side for us but just about affordable. I had a job working for the *South China Morning Post* as a down-table sub. Ruth was teaching English at the British Council. We had made the great move East: we had arrived: we had set ourselves up. We had done well. Slowly and subtly, the place began to drive me mad. Not Hong Kong but the flat.

Once you were out, it was hard to get in. This I could deal with, though it made me irritable. But once you were in, it was hard get out, and this began to play havoc with my mind. There were two lifts serving the building. It was too far to walk down the stairs, even if it could be done. It was common practice in Hong Kong to use the fire-stairs as the depository for all kinds of rubbish, preferably flammable. And of course, the metal gate at the bottom was always kept locked: well, anyone could walk in otherwise. Fire in Hong Kong tended to be a fairly total experience.

So it was the lift or nothing. And sometimes the lift came at once, but more often it didn't. You had to wait on the landing outside the flat for five, sometimes ten minutes. This oppressed me. Not just the waiting: more the fact that you couldn't walk out of your own house. It was as if outside was one place, inside quite another. There was no easy commerce between the two: instead, there was a massive transition to make, across a buffer zone, a no man's land, a DMZ between two irreconcilable opposites.

There was a cheerful shop across the road from our building and it sold everything, especially beer. Often enough, I would drop down to get a few cans and then come up again. The process sometimes took 20 minutes. The horizontal distance was about 60 feet. This was madness: not in the wasting of time, but in the vast and complex barrier that had been erected between inside and outside.

I loved Hong Kong. Right from the start, I felt absolutely at home: its madness found an answering chord in me. I was thrilled and challenged by its alien qualities; I found its bustle and its crowds hilarious. But the sense of being marooned 15 floors up, ten minutes away from outside, nibbled away at me. Once or twice, I made trips out to the outlying islands: to Lantau, Cheung Chau, Lamma. There I felt the sudden absence of traffic noise as a dramatic physical presence: the silence was an assault on the eardrums, making me quite literally feel dizzy, as if the silence had stirred up the semi-circular canals, the balance-regulating mechanism that lies in the inner ear. The extraordinary deep green of authentic tropical vegetation touched my soul: the entire world was full of pot plants, but without pots. I remember seeing the blue flash, dismayingly large, of a kingfisher of colossal size on a coastal walk. It released in me a huge yearning: to see more of the wild, yes, even to live on one of these wild islands. But I knew such a dream was impossible. I was a committed urbanite, was I not? Most nights I finished work at eleven, other nights at two: long after the ferries had stopped running. Besides, I was a townie. The countryside was something you visited, something that cheered you, that restored you and made possible your return to city life.

This problem was solved for me very neatly. I was sacked. I was penniless. I even owed money to the company. I was in shock. I was in debt. I was in shit.

So Ruth and I moved out to Lamma Island, sharing a flat with a colleague of hers, a delightfully eccentric Englishwoman called Sallie, who loved *The Sound of Music* above all other things in life, hated with a passion anything that might "make me think", and was given to exuberant public farting. I began to find work as a freelance, so that was all right. And I was at once at home in the pell-mell world of Lamma, the Chinese community of fishing people and market gardeners, and the floating, constantly changing population of multinational oddballs and misfits and bohos and drunks who washed up on the shores of the island.

The flat was on the ground floor. We seldom closed the door. Anybody could walk in. Anything. And did.

There was almost no difference at all between inside and outside. We had no air-conditioning, just a couple of fans bought from China Products to blow my papers about. I sat and drank coffee and beer inside or outside indifferently. The weather came right into the flat, just like everything else.

Ants marched in and out of the tiny kitchen in thin red

lines. Cockroaches had the run of the place in the dark: chunky, crunchy, chocolatey creatures with long antennae like, in Gerald Durrell's phrase, a mandarin's moustache. Mosquitoes materialised at dusk, mostly the little stripy kind, black-and-white house mosquitoes, practised tormentors. Translucent geckos appeared like magic to gobble them, bulbous eyes, internal organs visible beneath the skin, occasionally uttering a high-pitched giggle; the Malays give them the onomatopoeic name of *cheechak*. On one occasion, I found myself leaping naked onto Sallie's bed with Sallie inside it: her scream, more startled than frightened, had summoned me. A green praying mantis, body about three inches long, had settled on the cage that surrounded her fan, directly above her head. A little cravenly, I wrapped it in a tea towel rather than in my bare hands, and took it outside. Sallie thanked me gravely.

Naturally, everybody I met on the island regaled me with horror stories about wildlife, though nothing prepared me for the shock of my first serious encounter. Mostly, they talked about the centipedes: six inches long and ferociously fanged. The first that came my way was a rather adorable creature, to be quite frank. What was the fuss about? Six inches long and curling up like a liquorice all sort when touched with a broom, these could be gently whisked outside, where they would uncoil and get about their business. They weren't centipedes but millipedes, gentle vegetarians, creatures of great charm. There was a monstrous misidentification, I thought smugly.

I was wrong. The real centipedes, carnivorous and ferocious, came later. They moved with speed and sway-ing, wriggling purpose, and they could give you a most unpleasant bite. Not that I ever experienced one, though my friend Sam was bitten in the balls by one as he lay in bed. Still, he took worse things to his bed while he was on Lamma Island.

Sam was a New Zealander involved in advertising. He was loud, exuberant, cheerily foul-mouthed, in many ways a deeply silly man. For some reason, he was asked to front up one of his firm's television adverts. It was for a house-hold insecticide called Baygon. His light tenor was dubbed over with an authoritative American bass-baritone: but you could still imagine Sam's excited delivery behind: "You spray the fuckin' stuff all over the little bastards and it fuckin' kills 'em, yeah?"

The point of Baygon – the USP, Sam would say as an advertising man – was that the poison lay around for days after you had squirted it, killing everything that touched it. Quite serious stuff, then. But it had no effect on centi-pedes. Centipedes could be brushed out of the door, where there was every danger of them coming straight back in again, or they could, with considerable difficulty, be bro-ken with the back of a broom. I was surrounded by other houses, on a steep hillside, but with a 30-foot concrete wall at the back. Creatures frequently fell down this and couldn't get back up again. So they came into the house.

I was given my first serious test of my commitment to the island life by the huntsman spider. Now let me be frank: I don't care for spiders. Spiders give me the jumps. Why don't we get phobias about guns or ten-ton trucks, and other things that can seriously damage you? Instead, there are many people utterly terrified of the snakes they will never see, and bloody fools like me twitching at spiders that are damn-near harmless.

And God, that first one terrified the life out of me. I came back to the flat, alone, and found it on the wall. I couldn't believe it was so big. I suppose in legspan across the longest diagonal, it was six inches. It wasn't one of the furry bird-eaters of tropical forests, just a leggy wolf-spider, like the one you find in British gardens: agile, swift, not a web-maker but a great stalker and chaser and leaper. Magnified to an absurd degree.

It was in the bedroom. On the wall, like a monstrous plaque. Its stillness was filled with the threat of movement. It was altogether too much for me. I slept on the cushions in the sitting room that night. Alas, it was only the first: giant spiders came into the house on a dismayingly regular basis, and I had to deal with them or leave. At first, in fear and trembling, I Baygoned the fuckin' bastards, squirting so much stuff on them that they more or less dissolved on the wall, leaving me to sweep the soggy remains out with a finicky horror. But then a terrible thing occurred. I had two cats: one died of Baygon. My cleaning lady, distressed by the number of cockroaches (prey of the huntsman spider, as it happens) had a Baygon blitz. And the smaller of the cats, a dear creature who had few vices beyond the chewing of live cockroaches, ingested too much Baygon and died. So I banned Baygon, despite the cleaning lady's disapproval and Sam's nightly recommendations.

This meant that I had to reach an accommodation with living spiders. And this was nothing less than accommodation with nature. With the wild. It meant that I had to accept that nature was not all nice things. Nature was also things I didn't wish to stroke or encourage or invite back home. If you want nature, you have to have all of it: not just some of it. This was a dizzying concept. I knew that if I was to continue living on Lamma with my door open and no difference between inside and out, I had to live with six-inch wolf spiders.

By an effort of will, I did so. I still twitched when they moved without warning. I didn't like them. I wasn't brave enough to get rid of them. The only option was to accept them: to live alongside the creatures that peopled my nightmares. I ignored them: or rather, I mixed purposeful averting of my eyes with sudden gazes of horrified fascination. I wasn't happy with these many-legged giants: but I could live with them.

Many of the other visitors were welcome enough. Small frogs crept into the bathroom and sat there, looking oddly mournful, and as if carved out of soap. Giant cicadas slammed into the walls and into people as they manoeuvred with the grace of flying Volkswagens. Sometimes swarms of termites came zooming in towards the lights, shedding their wings recklessly all over the floor, leaving you with a dustpanful to sweep up after they had departed. Glorious butterflies thronged the few square feet of garden: dark-veined tiger and lemon.

I remember one afternoon with special vividness. I was working hard against a deadline on my electric typewriter, a machine I was inordinately proud of. I was wearing, as was my habit, nothing but a sarong tied insecurely around my waist, for I had gone native, gone bad in the Tropics, and very enjoyable it was, too. The flat was empty but for me and the two cats, for the little one was still alive then. The cats were making a terrible racket at my feet, and after a while I got a bit fed up with them and turned to ask politely: "Look, cats, could you please play a little more quietly?" But I only got halfway through.

On the floor, about six feet from my ankle, was a snake. I gasped: in shock, in horror, in wonder at the extraordinary beauty of the thing on the tiled floor, coiled up, its head ready to strike. It was a bamboo pit viper: green as poison with a red streak on the tail, yellow below, diamond-head much wider than the body, slim, about two feet long. It was utterly lovely. As I watched, Dinah, the bolder of the two cats, danced forward and slashed at it with her paw. She caught the snake on the side of its head and at once danced out of reach, as if she had some idea of what she was about. She had turned into Ricki-ticki-tavi.

Well, solve the moral dilemma for me. What's a person to do? A bamboo pit viper is, according to *A Colour Guide to Hong Kong Animals*, "not usually fatal to man". I liked that "usually". I knew that anybody who got bitten got helicoptered off the island: it's not a snake you take chances with. Bamboo pit vipers had been known to kill children and people with weak hearts.

Now here's an important truth about snake-bites: something like 98 per cent of all bites occur to people who are handling them. In my view, there's a fairly obvious negative suggestion implicit in that fact. I wasn't going to start handling this snake. So what were the other options? I could sweep it into the garden, from where it would come back into the flat. It certainly wouldn't climb back up the 30 foot wall, from which it had presumably and inadvertently descended. I could sweep it next door, into my landlord's garden. Or I could sweep it into either of my other neighbours' places. Not a neighbourly act, I think you'll agree.

So I killed it. I did it badly and uncoolly, but swiftly enough, two blows with the broom being enough to break its back and split its head. It was a desecration. I can see the mess I made of it now: I wish I couldn't.

Lamma was another Eden, and naturally, not without a

serpent or two. Others paid me visits, though I only had to take lethal actionon one other occasion, thank God. So if this was an idyll, it was one in which the difficulties, the ugliness, the danger, the ferocity and the fragility of life were always very clear. To believe that something is perfect is to demean it. To believe that something is perfect is, above all, an admission that you have failed to understand it. Perhaps that's why Ruth and I, after having established what I, at least, thought a perfect relationship, parted company. She went to live on the neighbouring island of Cheung Chau. I learned an awful lot of lessons about perfection while I was living on Lamma Island.

11. Little cormorant
Phalacrocorax niger

The rest-house had run out of beer. It might have been a disaster, but I saved the day. I happened to have with me a bottle of arrack, the indigenous Sri Lankan spirit. That's how I met Bob; that's how my life changed. We both wanted beer, I offered him a glass of arrack, he accepted. It was a fork in the road: once the decision had been reached and I had been taken, more or less been frog-marched onto the path less travelled by, there was no going back. And that made all the difference.

This strange and unexpected journey began, bizarrely enough, with a visit to Sam, my cockroach-killing friend from Lamma Island. I had business in town one Saturday, and finished a little before noon. I had an inspiration: Sam usually worked on Saturday morning, so I would collect him and buy him a beer, and then he would buy me a beer and then I would buy him a beer: and so a pleasant afternoon was in prospect for us both.

I had this brilliant idea as I was passing the building on Hong Kong Island that housed the office of his advertising company, so rather than telephoning, I took the lift up. It being a Saturday, there was no receptionist, so I opened the office door in a matey fashion and asked for Sam. He wasn't there. Ah well, never mind, I could always buy my own beer. I said farewell and turned to leave. "Aren't you Simon Barnes?"

I admitted that this was the case. "Would you be interested in doing some work for us?" I was a freelance writer: I was interested in doing work for anyone on any subject for 50 cents a word minimum. They had a contract with Korean Airlines: would I write some copy for their inflight magazine? Nine 500-word profiles on Asian cities?

Not a problem. I had even been to six of the cities. In this bustling metropolis, ancient and modern exist side by side. I could do that.

75 cents a word?

And I left.

By the time the lift hit the ground floor, I realised I had missed a trick. This was a bloody airline contract, after all, and airlines have bloody aeroplanes. I ran my eye down the list of nine cities. It rested on one of the three I hadn't been to. Colombo. I called back up from the phone in the lobby: "How about a barter deal?"

"What had you in mind?"

"Two return tickets to Sri Lanka."

So we went. Me and Cindy. Cindy my – to put this briefly – love, my wife, my life, mother of our children, my for-all-time companion and friend. At this stage we had known each other a few weeks, but I knew more or less all of those things already. And so we spent a few more weeks arguing and laughing and loving our way round the lovely and troubled island of Sri Lanka.

By the time we reached the beerless rest-house, we had been there for some time. When we felt in need of a treat, we stayed at a rest-house: places that had been built for colonial chaps to spend the night and take tiffin and a noggin or two when up-country. These buildings had an airiness and spaciousness that you don't find in places designed for air-conditioning, not that we could afford to stay in places that had air-conditioning. Even a rest-house was push-the-boat-out time, but we had decided that we deserved it on this occasion. It was an epochal decision.

There were two other guests, both English, a man and a woman, travelling independently. Bob was, I suppose, in his early 60s, and possessed of all the gregariousness of a man who lived and travelled alone. He was an unstoppable talker, and even before we spoke, I liked him hugely, because of the zillion watts of good cheer he was firing out in all directions. That's why I offered the drink. The woman was maybe ten years younger, quietly capable, a good and experienced traveller. I overheard the exchange with the waiter as she and Bob requested beer and the dreadful news came back.

So I came to the rescue. I explained that panic could be avoided: we could order bottles of soft drinks, politely insisting that the glasses and the bottles came separately. We could then mix the soft drinks with dia-mond-hard arrack in whatever proportions we chose. We ordered soda, ginger ale, lemonade. I passed around the arrack. We did it again, and then again. Bob grew expansive.

One of the things that had attracted me to Bob and prompted me to make the offer of arrack was that his conversation with the largely – and necessarily – silent companion kept returning to the subject of birds. It was clear that the subject consumed him. I had already heard him fix a wake-up call for six the following morning, with a pot of tea, please, so he could get in an hour's birdwatch-ing before the day got going. I admired this.

Laughing, gesticulating, between serious pulls at his arrack and soda, Bob talked about his travels in Sri Lanka and the birdwatching he had done. In particular, he expanded on the marvellous place he had been to the pre-vious day. It was called Gal Oya. It sounded wonderful. It sounded like paradise. So naturally, I didn't want to go. I loved hearing about it, loved Bob's easy familiarity with the wild world, but there was no way I was going to Gal Oya.

I think now it was because I didn't want to be disappointed. I didn't want to see it from the outside: to be there and yet not there, involved yet cut off from the essential meaning of the experience, much as I had been in my 15th-floor flat. I didn't want to do it wrong. I didn't know, but I already sensed that it was too important. Too important to risk getting wrong: almost too important to do.

But we went. Cind, who has been right about a million other things since then, said we should go, so we did. We managed to hire a pair of binoculars in Colombo, and then we set out on a small tour of the wild places of Sri Lanka. Starting, because Bob had made it sound so essential, with Gal Oya. A couple of days later, we were making our way towards a small boat, me filled with all kinds of trepidation.

The thought that it might be a false experience was almost too much to bear. The idea that I might be close to what I wanted without actually doing it right overwhelmed me. It was as if I had spent my life dreaming about the perfection of a cathedral, and, having finally arrived at its steps, feared to enter, in case it was filled with impious mobs selling postcards; or had spent years thinking about a great beauty spot but feared to go there in case I found nothing but parked coaches and McDonald's wrappers.

But it was not really the other people that worried me.

It was me. And it. Perhaps I would not respond to the wild world as I had when I was young. Perhaps the wild world was not as wonderful as I had always secretly believed. Perhaps I was not suitable for the wild world; perhaps the wild world was not suitable for me. I remembered the serial disappointments recounted by Proust: how the church in the Turkish style at Balbec was not the brave, wave-lashed cliff-top thing of beauty he imagined but a neat little spot in the middle of town; how Venice was somehow less Venetian that he had always dreamed. For Proust, real life was always a disappointment after the joys of the imagination, or the deeper joys when the past wells up without being summoned and all things fall into place. Perhaps I would be disappointed by the wild world: perhaps I was doomed to an inauthentic experience.

I had always imagined that somehow, all things would fall into place when I at last entered the wild world. It was fear that all things might not do anything of the kind that kept me away for so long. Now Cindy and I were walking with two Sri Lankans, a boat-driver and a spotter, towards the boat that lay moored on the shores of the vast artificial lake: an unreal — in fact man-made — and distinctly Tolkienesque landscape, dominated by a forest of drowned trees. Three rivers had been dammed to create this reservoir: the watery vista, the islands — formerly mere hills — and the landscape of the shores that made up the park.

The unreal nature of the waterscape added to its air of

mystery. The driver yanked the cord, the engine started. God, the sound would drive away every living thing for miles; this was just a joy-ride, a speedboat skirmish through a funky landscape, a cheap thrill. The driver throttled back, and we put-putted gently into the trees.

And entered a new space. Oh, brave new world that has such cormorants in it!

For – instantly, melodramatically, absurdly, suddenly – we made a transition from wild to tame. At once we were not near but inside a vast unending colony of birds. Every branch of every tree – bare, water-killed and slowly rotting – bore a cluster of strange black fruit. It was like looking at the stars on a frosty night: endless constellations and nebulae and galaxies of cormorants. Some were attending to their feathers with dandified precision, others struck the traditional heraldic pose of cormorant kind – the correct term is *displayed*, as in the spread eagle. These cormorants are correctly described as *cormorant sable displayed*, *wings inverted*.

They flew, they fished all around us, they squabbled, they dived. The stench of the whitewashed trees rose around us, and it smelt good to me. I had no idea that there were, in fact, three species of cormorants here: the dominant one being the little cormorant, a cheery, indomitable creature that loves to gather in huge numbers whenever there is enough water and enough fish. There were also great cormorants, the same species you find in Britain, and

Indian cormorants. But it was the lure of numbers that got to me on this first complete immersion into the wild world: so many! The fact of biodiversity – a term not yet invented – was the secondary experience. But it was still a matter of great wonder to notice that the darter, with its snaky neck, was quite different from the cormorants, and that of the many long-legged birds gathered around the edges of the lake, there were many different kinds: egrets, herons, night herons, painted storks. There were pelicans: I had no idea what species, or for that matter, no idea there was more than one. There were eagles, too: white-bellied sea-eagle and grey-headed fishing eagle, not that I really cared: I was simply drunk with the thought of being in the same place as eagles, my heart soaring as eagles soar, my imagination with it.

The spotter spotted elephant, far off, and we made our way towards the island they were standing on; here, the elephants swim from island to island, snorkelling with their trunks. I felt no great excitement at this: rather, a feeling that now we had entered the wild world, nothing, no matter how strange, no matter how beautiful, no matter how terrifying, no matter how wild, could cause me surprise. I was in a trance. I had finally reached the place where I wanted to be: the place I had conjured up a thousand times in the playground of Sunnyhill School, the place I had seen on the television with *Zoo Quest* and *Look*, the land I had sought in the Natural History Museum, the place I had pursued without knowing it ever since.

I had entered: and I knew already that there was no going back. I knew that henceforth, the wild world would be a major part of my life. I had no idea how to organise this, or what to do about it, barring an almost incontinent urge to write something about Gal Oya. I just knew that this was not so much a door as a valve, one that allowed you in but did not operate in the reverse direction. I had entered through the Wardrobe: but now the back of the Wardrobe was sealed for ever. I knew I would look at the world in a different way, understand life in a different way, live in a different way. I didn't know how or when or why: I didn't even care. All I knew was that I was back: back in a place I had never been to before, back in a place I had never truly left.

12. Marsh harrier
Circus aeruginosus

I always like to say that seeing a marsh harrier was the high spot of my honeymoon, though sometimes I vary it by saying that in fact, it was the morning I bought the thermal underwear. However, to be perfectly honest, there were some other good bits as well, though I still think I must have been mad to agree to it. Well, I was mad: mad about Cind. And that last sentence is in the wrong tense, but never mind. Where was I?

We came back to Lamma Island from Sri Lanka after a couple of months of adventures, and we had saved the best till last. The trip around the wildlife sites of Sri Lanka changed the island for us. It also changed Lamma, and as we went on, we discovered that it had changed everywhere else as well.

Lamma was suddenly strewn with birds. Where had they come from? I remembered *The Magician's Nephew*, the book in which the magical land of Narnia is created before the eyes of the observers, the animals rising from the earth itself – "Can you imagine a stretch of grassy land bubbling like water in a pot?... in all directions it was swelling into humps. They were of very different sizes, some no bigger than molehills, some as big as wheelbarrows, two the size of cottages. And the humps moved and swelled till they burst, as the crumbled earth poured out of them, and from each hump there came out an animal." After that "showers of birds came out of the trees" while frogs burst into the rivers and butterflies and bees appeared from nowhere. I remembered, too, the creation story in *Paradise Lost*, the egg bursting with kindly rupture, and the smaller birds that solaced the woods and spread their painted wings. The return to Lamma put us, rather unexpectedly, into the first chapter of the book of Genesis, and the fowls of the air were created before us, for surely, they had not been there before. But now they were everywhere and, it sometimes seemed, they were there for me alone. This was at first something to plume myself on, secondly a privilege. These days it also feels like a responsibility.

But first came the joy: and the joy has never left. The scrap of garden before our flat called into new being three species of bulbuls: most notably the crested bulbul, an absurd little bird got up like a clown, with red cheeks and a pointed hat. The Chinese bulbul, with a head like a badger, made a shocking din I had never heard before: but now it did it every morning. There was also a red-vented bulbul: how did that get there? How come I had never seen the magpie robin, as jaunty a little bird as exists anywhere in the world? Where had they all come from? I discovered them with the help of Karen Phillips who illustrated *A Colour Guide to Hong Kong Birds*, the first bird book I had acquired deliberately since I had won the great field guide by learning the multiplication tables.

Of course, I already knew about the black kites that drifted across the skies of Hong Kong and sometimes delicately plucked stuff from the water's surface as the ferry chugged to and from Lamma. I had often seen them wheeling about the peak, flapping seldom, twisting their forked tails to steer. But I was shocked to find that some of these kites were in fact white-bellied sea eagles, yes, and there was a strange sense of appropriateness in discovering that this was the same eagle I had seen at Gal Oya. It was part of a pleasing pattern: and I have been falling on pleasing patterns like that ever since. And just a few weeks before, this eagle hadn't even existed. There had been one kind of big bird: and now there were two. It was as if I had split the atom, sundered like from like and created two unlikes. The eagle carried its wings in a shallow vee, a dihedral, and was altogether more chunky and substantial an aeronaut.

And the sparrows that cheeped around the house: it was with a shock that I realised that these were not house sparrows at all. Rather, they were tree sparrows, which I knew about from my studies with S Vere Benson: country cousins of the cockney sparrow, birds that habitually have nothing to do with buildings. They had a fine chestnut head, rather than the ashy grey of the house sparrow, something I had never noticed before. But now we were sudden intimates.

There were other, more exotic birds leaping from nowhere: rufous-backed shrike, blue rock thrush, white-breasted kingfisher, no doubt the large blue bird that had given me such delight in a previous life. You could see reef egrets from the ferry, sometimes great rafts of red-necked phalarope in the Lamma Channel. Once a great frigate bird flew over the island: impossibly slim wings, deeply forked tail. I made an expedition to an egretry: two or three huge trees among the branches of which the long-legged birds looked like giant white fruit. Sometimes the call of the koel echoed across the island, saying its own name, though I preferred to think that it sounded like my friend Al when lit up by enthusiasm and Carlsberg: "Un-*real*! Un-*real*!"

But the bird that gave me most pleasure in this time of Creation was a little thing that I saw every day. That's to say, I now saw it every day. Very close to the harbour wall was a large boulder: that was its regular perch. Every day, on ten separate occasions, 500 people would pass within ten yards of it going towards the ferry pier and then 500 more would come the other way as they left the ferry for the delights of the island. And the bird, which I had always believed to be the most shy and elusive of all birds, would never twitch a feather. Instead, it would sit there, bobbing its head, glaring at the surface of the sea, occasionally turning itself into an iridescent dart and flying at the water, to return to its favourite perch on the boulder to scoff a tiddler.

It was a kingfisher. One of the most sought-after and beloved of birds, an outrageous explosion of colour, the bird everybody wants to see: and yet nobody saw it. Nobody noticed because nobody looked. It had been there all the time, or at least I assumed so. But it was as if my awakened eyes had called it into being, summoned it from the rock as Aslan summoned the animals from the boiling ground in Narnia, as God called the birds to burst forth with kindly rupture in *Paradise Lost*. Perhaps it was the bird I most wanted to see: the bird with which everyone most craves an intimacy: and at a stroke, it was there for me every day. I nodded to it as I went to work; I waved to it when I returned to the island in daylight hours, generally as I was making my way to the bar.

I was drunk with delight: half-seas over on the joy of the things that the smallest adjustment of vision had brought before me. But it was not as if I had changed: it was more as if the world itself had changed, and done so especially to please me. It was as if things I longed to see had become visible before my eyes, as if the creatures I longed to share my life with had appeared, summoned by my own needs. The earth had changed: it had changed for me: and it would never change back. No wonder I was drunk.

We ended our Hong Kong adventures and returned to England. Cind was going through drama school; we had a bedsit in Ealing. I was doing sub-editing shifts for *Titbits*, and subbing the astrology for the *Daily Mail*. It was all rather suddenly and dramatically different from freebooting around Asia. The wild world went elusive again. But I was with Cind; what else mattered? I also began to write for *The Times*. I had nothing to complain about. We went ahead and got married while Cind was at college. What little money we had was in a building society awaiting some fantastical moment when we might be able to buy a little shitheap of our own. There was none to spare.

So Cind had the notion that we should spend our honeymoon on the Norfolk Broads. In April. Her family has always had romantic feelings about boats: Cind's mother spent the first seven years of her life at sea, while her grandfather had captained one of the last Thames sailing barges to run cargo around the coast of Britain. (He took it to and from Dunkirk several times during the great evacuation as well.) Cind chose a boat from a catalogue, one suitable to the grand-daughter of a sailing bargee. And me, I had forgotten what England was like. I had spent the last four years in Hong Kong and then the past eight months in offices, in the tube, in pubs, in the bedsit, which was warm enough if you had sufficient coins to appease the hunger of the meter. I was not prepared for this.

You couldn't fault the theory. We needed to see the horizon. We needed to be where wild things were. It was just so cold that I wanted to die. Still, we made that stop and bought that thermal underwear and things improved. And there were nice birds, even if I didn't really know how to look at them. Despite the best efforts of S Vere Benson and Roger Tory Peterson, I was a hopeless practical birdwatcher. Still, I had binoculars, and I peered at birds here and there, and very often, the sight of the bird would marry up with the half-remembered, wholly-loved images from *The Observer's Book of Birds* and from other books I had perused so often and so long and so fruitlessly.

I had once owned quite a few. People gave me bird books. Kind grandparents, kind aunts, kind friends of the family bought them for me. It was the default present. When in doubt, they gave me bird books: sometimes years after I had stopped thinking of myself as a birdwatcher. All kinds of unexpected memories from those days of nightly perusal came into play as we chugged our way around the Broads. We saw kingfishers, fleeting and distant, and congratulated ourselves on our field skills. I saw a tern, sitting on a post just as it did in a photograph in a book I could no longer name: but how much better this bird looked in its black-and-white reality than it did in its black and white picture, in those days when colour photography was an exoticism.

I remembered one such photograph with special clarity. It was in a book of black-and-white pictures, each picture accompanied by a brief text. It showed a male marsh harrier on a nest: I was to learn later that it was a famous picture taken by the great pioneer of bird photography, Eric Hosking. The bird stood there with his wings raised high like the wings of an angel: indeed, some claim that the carved angels in the churches of Suffolk are borne aloft on marsh harriers' wings. Alongside this bird is a chick of woeful ugliness. I no longer have the book in question, but I have a book of Hosking photographs, and it includes this seminal and dramatic picture, taken in 1942, when this was a feat of adventure on the far edge of the possibilities of technology.

I can't remember the wording of the caption in my original, but it basically said that if you want to see a bird like this, think again. This, it said, is a bird beyond your scope. It is a bird for supermen, a bird for the elite of the elite. It is only found in the wildest places, and it has been driven – harried – to the point of extinction. I couldn't know when I read the book as a boy, and I didn't know when I visited the Broads on my honeymoon, that the population of marsh harriers was reduced to a single breeding pair in 1971: that summer when I listened stoned to birdsong in the garden of Burwalls. All I knew was that marsh harriers were rare beyond all hope of ever seeing one.

And I saw one. Our barge-like boat was tied up, and since Cind sat there it was like a burnished throne that burnt on the water. Certainly, its occupant beggared all description. And so, for that matter, did something else I saw when I turned my eyes from the boat to see a large flying bird, unmistakably a bird of prey, yet not a black kite or a white-bellied sea eagle; or, to be a bit more English and sensible, clearly not a kestrel or a sparrow-hawk or a buzzard or any of the birds of prey you are allowed to see. It flew with the greatest nonchalance, hanging in the air as though doing the air a favour, holding its wings, a bit like the white-bellied sea eagle to tell the truth, in a shallow vee or dihedral. But it was the wrong shape for an eagle; it had the wrong vibes, and besides, it was the wrong place. I couldn't believe my eyes, or rather, my mind: I was convinced that I must have made the most colossal howler, that some obvious and common bird explained this fabulous and thrilling sight, that if I were to explain it to a proper birdwatcher, I would be laughed at: Oh, that's the sort of thing crows do round these parts; it's a well-known confusion. Did you really think you'd see a marsh harrier? That's too rich for words.

But it had to be. Didn't it? Eventually, almost to my relief, it floated easily away on whatever drifting errand that absorbed it, and I went back to the barge and the barge-borne queen, my long-johns warm beneath my trousers, to look it up. "Has *low quartering* flight with occasional wing-beats and long wavering glides, with wings in shallow vee." There was no questioning any further. A miracle had taken place before my eyes. The dead had been brought to life: the extinct had leapt up before me in glorious existence: the impossible was now quite obviously possible.

There were two endlessly thrilling things to deal with. The first was this dramatic revelation, this epiphany, which had informed me that the wild world is available to us all, even the likes of me; that impossible creatures were there for the seeing, that I didn't have to be a different person to do that seeing. All I had to do was look, and to be forever looking, and I would always be able to see. The wild was within my scope: within my reach: within my grasp.

The second was that nearly extinct is not the same as extinct: that imminent disaster is not the same as disaster. It was unquestionably true that marsh harriers had become fantastically rare in this country: but that was not the end of the matter. Things had changed. Things had, it seemed, improved. Things had actually got better: how about that for a thought? I didn't know then that DDT had been the problem, that it is a residual poison, that it builds up in all creatures in the food chain: that it builds up in the insect-eaters, and therefore the build-up builds up catastrophically in those that eat the insect-eaters. I didn't know that DDT causes eggshell-thinning in birds of prey, and so the eggs broke and bird after bird failed to breed. I didn't know that the poison was now illegal in this country, and that since it was banned, birds of prey had begun a recovery, aided by conservation organisations like the Royal Society for the Protection of Birds. The RSPB looks after many acres of reedbed, which is the prime habitat of marsh harriers.

What I did understand was that I had a legitimate cause for optimism. I could rightly feel optimistic about the world and optimistic about the possibilities it had. I felt that life was only now beginning in earnest: that the 30-odd years I had lived were nothing more than a preparation for the real thing that was now upon me. It was not a new start. It was the start. That's what honeymoon, that's what marriage means. A new optimism was sustained in the air: it had a *low, quartering* flight with occasional wing-beats and long wavering glides. Hope had taken to the air above me, holding its wings in a shallow vee.

13. Grey whale
Eschrichtius robustus

A few years after my return to England, the wedding, the honeymoon and the marsh harrier, I was, if I might be so immodest, a success. At least, modest aims had been immodestly realised. I was a sports columnist for *The Times*, I travelled to far places to write stories, I had won a journalistic award, I had published a couple of books. What more could anyone want?

Cind and I were now living in a Victorian terraced house built on the roof of a railway tunnel at the extreme northern tip of London – clinging onto town by a whisker – and she was working as an actress when the work came in. Things were going well, and there was plenty more still to be done, more than enough to give savour to life.

It was January and I had a trip before me. Its main

purpose was to cover the Super Bowl, the final game of the American football season. It was to take place in San Diego, and I had been told a fine thing about that town, something that lit up the prospect of the entire trip. I was also to go on from San Diego to Los Angeles to spend a few days at the racetrack doing some horsey stories; but before that I had to go to Atlantic City to cover some boxing. Mike Tyson was to fight Larry Holmes for the heavy-weight championship of the world.

I can only assume that the reason for my presence in Atlantic City was economy, for this was a drastic measure. Certainly, the boxing correspondent was far from pleased, but he showed no signs of blaming me for stealing his trip. He knew I hated boxing. I had covered a fight in Las Vegas, in the belief that every sportswriter must do so at least once, and I had loathed every inch of the place and every nuance of the event. I had also written fairly unapologetically in favour of the abolition of boxing. I was in no mood to start enjoying myself, then.

Atlantic City was vile, without any of the surrealism that – sometimes for minutes at a time – redeems Vegas from itself. Atlantic City was Las Vegas without the charm and sophistication; Las Vegas with all the subtlety and intellectual challenge removed; Las Vegas without the chance of escape. I walked endlessly along the winter boardwalk to get away from the claustrophobia of the gambling halls, past the same grey Atlantic that rolls past

England, squadrons of ring-billed and herring gulls wheeling and squabbling around my head, marching through the short days before twilight forced me to return to the hotel, the way to my room taking me not-at-all beguilingly past serried ranks of slot machines and gaming tables, back in the land where there is no night and no day.

I can't say I handled myself well in Atlantic City. I drank copiously with kind and generous colleagues in the bar known as the Irish bar, a place blessedly without gambling to distract you from the task of drinking, but that was not the problem. I began to feel increasingly peculiar. Before long it became clear that I was entering the arena of the unwell. I grew increasingly disconnected. When I spoke I could hear my own voice in my head, as if I was listening to myself on headphones. I remember disconcerting an American sportswriter who, out of sheer good manners, asked me my views on the coming Super Bowl and whether I favoured the Redskins or the Broncos. I told him that my real ambition was the whales. I hadn't intended to broach the subject, but sometimes you just say what you're thinking, particularly when disconnected.

I got through the fight all right. Better than Holmes, anyway. Got my copy written. It was a brutal business. In 1980, when Holmes had fought the fading Muhammad Ali, he had shown compassion, and refused to destroy the man before him. Tyson had no such instincts. *Au contraire.* He pummelled the beaten Holmes with sadistic relish over four bloody rounds. The crowd roared: it was clearly worth paying good money for such a spectacle. Afterwards, I did the press conference duties, my head spinning like a top. And all the time, very high, very faint, very distant, I could hear music. I wasn't humming to myself: the music was outside of me, or certainly seemed so: apparently wholly external in origin. I could recognise it, though: a tiny fragment from Paul Simon's then hugely popular album, *Graceland*. It played on and on, on an endless loop: "I don't *want* no part... I don't *want* no part... I don't *want* no part..."

I went back to my room – reeled, rather – and soaked the sheets with my sweat, abandoning them towards dawn, cold and clinging, for prickly but dry blankets. Then, after a weekend in New York, mostly spent sweating and starving and drinking water, I took myself, recovered and again cheerful, free from both flu and the sulks, across the continent to San Diego, there to immerse myself in the madness of the Super Bowl, to take part in the massed press conferences and the press breakfasts for 2,000, to climb the cholesterol mountain of scrambled eggs, to pile into the media scrimmages at those times when all the players were available and the linebackers and the nose tackles and the free safeties all politely told us what sort of tree they would be. Super Bowl week is so absurd it makes cynicism redundant. No one believed in it as a serious occasion: everyone went along with it. There was absolutely no danger whatsoever of confusing this with reality. It all made great copy, of a not uncrazy kind, and I was content throughout, if not entirely sober of an evening.

But all along, it was Saturday I was looking forward to. The game, I should point out, was Sunday.

I had walked up and down the waterfront at San Diego every day, for sunlight in winter is a rare and precious thing for an English soul. And there I found what I was looking for, and so I paid my money – five bucks? Ten bucks? Maybe even 20? No matter, it was a wonderful investment. Saturday morning came, and I made my way out for the treat with all the other tourists, as if we were making a journey to the lighthouse rather than a pilgrimage towards ultimate truth. Most of my fellow-passengers, my fellow-Ishmaels, were people in town for the big game, some wearing grotesque colours to show their scarlet or orange affiliations, others wearing the curious clothes Americans wear for lee-zhurr, most with children, because we all know that the wild world is a thing for children, rather than grown-ups. There were even a couple of my colleagues: I had obtained tickets for them at their request, for they showed unexpected enthusiasm when I mentioned my plan, and I was, even then, not without an evangelical streak. One of them, Simon Kelner, went on to edit the *Independent*, and under his leadership, the paper became notable for the prominence given to stories on wildlife and the environment.

But on with the trip. A slow trudge out to sea, cheerful yammering of families on a day out, endlessly taking pictures of the boat and each other, other vessels around us, boats that were following us to steal our captain's knowledge and expertise and gain a free look at the treasures we were tracking.

And we found them. We found them all right. A pod of three grey whales: I simply couldn't believe it. I mean that quite literally: this was not a thing that made for easy credibility. It was, unlike the Super Bowl press conferences, quite evidently real, but something in the mind rejected the evidence of the senses. This couldn't be, could it? These things, so uncompromisingly, so bewilderingly huge: they couldn't exist just like that, could they? It didn't make any sense to our human, our land-locked, our city-locked gaze. I stared at the three plumes of spume, each one holding a distinct shape for a couple of seconds before being whipped away in the sprightly breezes of the ocean. A back, breaking the surface, then rolling, siphoning past us, also like an endless loop, on and on, more and more and more of it, yard after yard after yard. Then a pause and then again the breaking, the echoing sigh of the triple breaths: the grey whales southing their way towards the breeding lagoons of Baja California.

That breathing is the most colossally intimate thing: the vast noise – grey whales are noted for the din of their blow

– the least subtle way possible of reminding us that whales are mammals, just like us, that they breathe, just like us, and for that matter, they drown, just like us. Some scientists have suggested that sometimes the whales that get beached are sick animals, returning to land in dread of death by drowning. To see a whale is to experience not differences but similarities: not what divides us but what we share.

After that, the sounding. A deeper sigh, a more explosive exhalation/inhalation, the body siphons past, perhaps a shade more quickly, and certainly there is more of it than before, for it takes longer to go past and then – oh, like a Roman candle bursting – the flukes break the surface and the great grey Y is silhouetted against the sky, dripping, wonderfully elegant in shape and conception, and then soundlessly it has vanished. Who could restrain a gasp, an oath, a tear? I wanted to drop to my knees, sing hallelujahs, fling myself into the ocean, kiss all the prettiest girls on the boat, the plain ones too, utter broken thanks to the skipper, be for ever a better, a humbler, a wiser person.

When the flukes break the surface – that's when the differences come crashing home, the extraordinary fact that these creatures are so much bigger than us, for all their likeness so unlike us, for all the received wisdom of their near-human intelligence, so fundamentally at odds with any way of thinking that humans can grasp. Fellow-mammals: creatures as alien as any a science-fiction writer ever came up with: these were the denizens of Mars, Krypton, Tralfamadore, yet they were equipped with flesh and blood and lungs and hearts like our own. It was the scientist and writer JBS Haldane who said: "My own suspicion is that the universe is not only queerer than we suppose, but queerer than we *can* suppose." You don't have to leave the atmosphere of the earth to know that he's right.

Every time the flukes broke the surface was a profound revelation of this truth. We were face to face with the vastness of whales, the vastness of creation, the vastness of the principles that make our planet function. There was no song in my head save the sighing of the whale's breath. I wanted to be a part of it – but then I was a part of it, after all, and had been all along. That was inescapable. The great Y in the sky said Yes, and Yes, and Yes again.

Eventually we left them: whales in the process of making the longest migration known to mammals: 10,000 miles from the Arctic to Baja and back again, 20,000 of them doing it every year. They used to make a similar journey in the Atlantic as well, but the whalers put paid to that: the grey whale went extinct in the Atlantic as early as the 17th century.

The game the following day was good, or at least it was a damn good story; Washington Redskins, the first team to make the Super Bowl with a black quarterback, beat the Denver Broncos 42-10. On Monday I caught the plane for the short hop north up the coast to LA. For some reason, I had a window seat; I normally prefer an aisle, but perhaps I asked for a window for once. Perhaps I already had a plan to look at the ocean from a dizzy height. Certainly that's what I did, sipping rather than gulping a cold beer that stung the palate agreeably, staring down at the wrinkled sea and wondering how many whales swam and rolled beneath its grey-blue surface. That's the thing about whales: the conjuring trick: one minute there is just sea; and then, like a Brobdingnagian rabbit from a horizon-filling hat, comes the whale. That something so immense could appear from nowhere is gloriously unsettling, going against all kinds of preconceptions. It seems so utterly unnatural: and at the same time, the most natural thing in the world. That's the stunningly obvious contradiction that gets to everyone who sees a great whale: that combination of complete astonishment and complete inevitability: of total disbelief and perfect confirmation.

The sea is only alive for us at the surface. All that lies beneath is invisible, inaudible, unimaginable: non-existent, until it forces itself on our attention. We have no conception of what life is like down there, in the aqueous depths; we can't begin to comprehend how it feels to make a 5,000-mile underwater trek between Arctic and Baja, to make that endless, endlessly repeated journey from A to B and back again. We just see something that breaks the surface: it appears, it materialises: we can't really come to terms with the idea that it was there all along: and then it is gone again, as baffling as before.

And with their immensity, their fragility. No group of creatures has come to represent the fragility of the earth as much as the whale. In a thousand campaigns across the 70s and 80s, the notion of Saving the Whale was a revelation of the lurking secret immensities of our world, and of the human genius for destruction, a thing still more immense. To view a whale in his might is to see the planet as a thing of perfect fragility.

I looked down over the water pondering such matters: the sea, yes, the dominion of the whales, the kingdom of whales, the – no, come on, the *principality* of whales, that's more like it. And I found, as not seldom before, that my response to something immense was to try and write it. I wanted to write those whales. After all, I was a writer, was I not? True, I had written over the past fortnight of Holmes and Tyson and Washington Redskins and Denver Broncos – and also of hate and violence and mercy and race and prejudice and its conquest – but now, I wanted to write these whales. My whales: perhaps I wanted to capture them in the only way I could, to harpoon them with my prose, and thereby to order the turmoil they had raised in my mind. It was, I suspect, an instinct I shared with most of the on-board dads whose need to capture the whales in a photograph was something I mildly despised. We all need not only to see but somehow to claim: above all, to achieve some kind of union.

I wanted to write whales. I wanted to write nature. I wanted to write beasts and birds, I wanted to write wild, I wanted to write my delight, I wanted to tell the world how to savour and to save the great beasts I had just seen.

A few hours later I was at Santa Anita racetrack with a pass that took me to the stables and the horses and the grooms and the work-riders and the hot-walkers and the trainers and all the backstage intimacies of American racing, and I had the opportunity to spend getting-on-for-a-week lurking around and meeting some of the greatest men and horses taking part. I had a wonderful time and got some half-decent stories as well. And all the time, very faint and distant, I could still hear music, the music of the whales' breath. It was a summoning.

It's not that sport wasn't enough. I loved writing about sport: I still do. I have never written much about tactical nuances or transfer sagas: rather, for me, sport is a window into humanity. For me, for all sportswriters, whether they choose to acknowledge it or not, their subject is not sport but humanity. Sport shows us such things as, well, hate and violence and mercy and race and prejudice and its conquest and a thousand other things as well. The sportswriter is uniquely privileged among newspaper journalists: because in competition, the athlete can't help but reveal himself. I had, and have no wish to give up writing about sport. But it is not enough. Not because sport is not enough, but because humanity is not enough.

14. Garden warbler
Sylvia borin

I held the giggling, naked girl close. She was, I think, Chinese. She giggled again, more loudly this time, in a manner that took me back just a little. I was not yet to know then that she would drive me mad, obsess me, possess me, persuade me to take ridiculous risks with my marriage and my professional life. She giggled once again, and I was aware that all was not well. There was something amiss with the giggle. With that realisation, she began to fade, her lovely naked self vanishing inside the enfolding arc of my arms, until, like the Cheshire Cat, only the giggle remained. I was awake now, the sound of the giggle echoing down from the trees above.

The air was full of strange sounds, sounds I had never heard before. I put together the events of the previous night: the long flight, 17 hours delayed, the journey in the dark, all of us crammed into the Land Cruiser, the occasional bizarre sight of a nightjar caught in the headlights. Then the short night, and an awakening through the giggles to a morning concert of still stranger sounds. I had entered a land of enchantment, and from the first I was lost.

I was in the Kafue National Park in Zambia, inhabiting a soundscape that was loud, potent and unfamiliar. It was the sounds that seized me from the first: my hearing, leaping well beyond the walls of my hut and the limits of my vision, greedily gathered information from all points of the compass. Not that I was able to analyse, still less understand that concert: it was a savage jumble with no order and no meaning. I was adrift in a strange sea of sound; I had no point of reference and nothing much to float on save my own sense of wonder.

It was much later that I worked out that the sound of the giggling girl came via a red-eyed dove, a bird with a curious and rhythmic coo, sometimes interpreted as "three cheers for the BBC". But, still unknowing, I emerged from my dream and then from my hut, but never once, for the duration of that trip – nor for many years afterwards – did I emerge from the trance of wonder in which I had awoken that first morning.

It was not just my first day in Africa. It was also the day I stopped looking at wildlife. Before that day, experiencing wildlife had been a bit like watching television: it was as if there was a sheet of glass between me and it. I was slightly cut off from everything. Locked up inside a single sense, I was an outsider looking in, wanting to belong but forever separate, like the character in *The Rainbow* looking through the window at the woman he loves. But Africa has a way of taking people beyond their limitations. Africa forced itself on every sense I possessed: compelling me without my volition into a five-dimensional view of the world. I was, at a stroke, an omni-directional, multi-layered, pen-tangled human, Leonardo's Vitruvian man with binoculars round my neck, ears aflap and every sense at last awake. The smell of Africa hits everyone. It is beyond analysis: a touch of burn, a hint of spice, a mix of a million other trace elements, a strange nose-tingling curry. The sense of smell is so closely allied to taste that the scent of Africa becomes almost esculent in the heady occasions when you leave the vehicle and walk in the bush, between thorn-bushes and lions, over the neat sugared-almond tracks of antelopes and around the great loaves of elephant dung. Everything feels thrillingly unfamiliar: the grass that swishes at your ankles, the dragon-scale bark of the mopane trees, the smooth surface of the kigelia trees, called sausage tree for their extraordinary fruit, the popa-dum crunch of the super-dried leaves beneath your feet. The sights astounded me. But it was the sounds that had me, in the immortal words of Brendan Behan, bewitched,

142

bollixed and bewildered.

I remember the cheerful quarrelsome noise of a baboon colony interrupted by a shattering double bark from one vast male, suddenly standing, however precariously, on his hind legs: how others took it up and though I knew nothing of African wildlife or bush-lore, I instantly understood that something astonishing was about to happen. So there, on my first morning in Luangwa Valley, the other side of Zambia from Kafue, a leopard and her cub appeared in full daylight. In my trance I was hardly aware of our luck: I assumed such wonders were available every day, on every such morning in which the world was made new once again.

It was Baron Robert Stjernstedt who first began to isolate individual sounds for me. How shall I describe the Baron? Bob has given his life to the sounds of African birds, making recordings of 571 species in Zambia alone. He was working as a safari guide when I first met him on that unforgettable trip: a mad figure with mended glasses, ragamuffin shirt with patch-pockets with far too many things in them, shorts the crotch of which was a crochet pattern of holes made by burning shards of tobacco from his smouldering roll-ups. I used him as a model for a character in my first novel, *Rogue Lion Safaris*, but (like the flat in *Withnail and I*) I toned him down to make him believable. I have since had a number of extraordinary and potentially lethal adventures with Bob, not least the time when we nearly got squashed by a train on a bridge in Wales. Bob began the process that released me from mere vision. Thanks to Bob, I became less of an observer, more a participant. I remembered Bob and the scimitarbill: a dark, elegant, long-tailed bird related to the hoopoes with a beak to match its name. It is a great whistler. Bob engaged it in dialogue by whistling back. Each time Bob whistled, the scimitarbill replied. Bob daringly changed the pitch of his whistle: and the bird responded, changing to tune in with Bob. There was less division between human and non-human out to here in the bush. It was a marvellous first lesson, but the second was still more marvellous. This principle, once established, could be carried out into the wider world.

I never left the Luangwa Valley. I took it away with me, leaving in exchange a small piece of my heart. And as I returned home, so I began to encounter wildlife in a different way. I was no longer a mere looker. You can't entirely recreate the sensation of standing in the African sun with a beer in your hand and a pride of lions a hundred yards away, not in Hertfordshire, anyway, but you can bring home the lesson learned. This is not a lesson you learn like the multiplication tables: rather, it is something you become aware of almost without knowing it. It is, if you like, a matter of changing your mind: not in the sense of choosing to do or believe in something else, but in the sense that your mind itself is altered. Oh, I tried to alter my mind with drugs in those brief dizzy days in Room Six, but I was never much in love with the means or the process. Africa had hit me with the force of a million-mike acid trip, and this time, I had no thought of resisting. Holding onto my essential sanity was no longer the preferred option. One of the supposed pleasures of the hallucinogens is the opening up of the senses: Ralph feeling every blade of grass, me listening to the birds of Burwalls. But Africa triggered in me a response far deeper, imbued with far more meaning. My senses were not so much exaggerated as keyed in: I was aware of them, and I was aware of what they sensed as never before. The wild world spoke to me, entering through every sensory portal.

I was, then, by the time I got to Minsmere, awakened. It was here I met Jeremy Sorensen, who took me through the next door. Jeremy was chief warden of the RSPB's nature reserve at Minsmere, in Suffolk, and I was writing a book about a year in the life of the place, for, strange to tell, I was now a wildlife writer, or at least, I had a commission to write a book about wildlife. Every week I would leave my north-north-London fastness and take a train north and east from Liverpool Street, changing to the rattler at Ipswich. From Saxmundham, a taxi took me to Minsmere, and there I did my research. Some of it was walking and talking, but an awful lot more was sitting about with my mouth agape. The most important thing was listening: to Jeremy, to the others who worked on the reserve, and crucially, to the birds themselves.

I had been to Minsmere before. I had spent some enchanted days there with Cind, and we had shared vivid encounters with, among others, kingfishers and marsh harriers. The RSPB had tried to steer me away from Minsmere, because it was famous enough already. But I wanted Minsmere because Minsmere had something special: it had that sense of privilege. It seemed – no, it was – the case that at Minsmere, birds reduced their flight distances. They let humans get closer than they did outside. They had less fear, because the humans they encountered were 100 per cent benign. If you skyline yourself in most low-lying places, you will put the birds to flight: at Minsmere, you can do so without concern. On my first visit a wren took to the top of a small bush and sang his song five yards away from me. Though I saw some fabulous exoticisms that day, this was perhaps the enduring image of the place: a skulking bird flaunting himself in full view of a human. I was no longer a source of fear: I was treated, by a bird, as a belonger.

It was crucial to establish a good relationship with Jeremy, but that presented no difficulties. Not that Jeremy was by any stretch of the imagination a straightforward fellow. He was, in his way, as rum a bugger as the Baron. Jeremy was one of those clever men who had never been over-educated. He had to find it all out as he went along: he had been an effective manager of a chain of shops, while doing a great deal of work ringing birds as a volunteer. He had then cast aside his worldly ambitions in the retail trade and joined the RSPB as a warden, ending up steering the flagship. Affable, Lancastrian, quirky, eccentric, given to unexpected mental leaps, he had taken Minsmere from being a place that was kept cut off, almost secret, almost paranoically wary of visitors, to something not entirely unlike a tourist trap: save that those trapped were not fleeced but given something that could last them the rest of their lives. That is to say, birds; that is to say, the wild world. Minsmere now has a shop and tea-room and a daily year-round invasion of visitors. This is Jeremy's great achievement: and since he left, the traditions he established have been continued and expanded.

"How good are you on your song and call?"

This was one of Jeremy's first questions to me, and I had to confess that I was hopeless. Not even a beginner, for I had no idea where to start. I had always thought that birdsong was something, well, a bit soppy, a bit girly, a bit unnecessary, like pressing wild flowers. True, with Bob, I had learned the sound of red-eyed dove, also of African fish eagle and wood owl and one or two others. But back at home, I could scarcely tell a crow from a blackbird. I didn't even try.

Jeremy continued where Bob had left off: give him a sound, and, like a magician, he produced a bird. Picture me, then, moving from platform to platform at Ipswich station, boarding the rattler to Saxmundham, finding my window seat and cramming the headphones back over my ears, switching on the Walkman to listen, once again, to my tape of the birds of Minsmere, bought in the Minsmere shop. Again and again I played the tape, hoping that I too would become a magician. Hoping to expand my senses, alter my mind, change my world.

I remember with almost perfect vividness the day that I did so. I was out censusing birds with Rob Macklin, then Jeremy's assistant, now Suffolk area manager. Rob was burly, bearded, once a more than useful cricketer, and a Bothamesque all-rounder as a field naturalist. Censusing has always been his passion: despite his elevated administrative role, he still sneaks off with his maps and his notebooks and his sharpened pencils every time he can get away.

It was the repetition of the real birds that finally got through to me, because Rob stopped to write down every bird he heard. That was the point of the trip, after all. So every time he heard a willow warbler, he stopped and wrote down "willow warbler", and every time he did so, I heard the silvery liquid trickle of notes, lisping down the scale, and before very long, I knew that I would always know a willow warbler whether I saw it or not. We came across a little sun-washed hollow full of brambles: here was whitethroat heaven, a perfect habitat for these neat little warblers, and because the shelter and the food supplies were optimal, the birds were there in intense profusion. We counted six of them in a brake you would circle in half a minute: and I knew, again, that the brief, intense, scratchy sound was locked in my mind, and that I would never hear a whitethroat in full song without knowing it for what it was.

All this I took home from Minsmere and tried, falteringly, to put into practice for myself. Alas, the seasons went too fast for me. The year turned, and autumn was on us, and the big singing was over by the time I was getting the hang of it. I recall standing on a train station – Welwyn North, I think – with the leaves already turning and the autumn soloist in full song, and I wanted to shake everybody waiting for the train: "Listen! That's a bloody robin! And it's wonderful! Got it?"

When the singing began again the following spring, I was at last able to put myself to the test. One by one, like a man building a wall, I began to construct my edifice of birdsong: the repeating song thrush, the limpid blackbird, the morsing great tit, the trilling wren, the soaring song of the soaring skylark. Then I began to add the migrants as they arrived and began to sing in their turn: the chiming chiffchaff, the willow warbler returning both to England and to me, and then the whitethroat, his song remembered by himself and, to my immense delight, by me as well.

And a bird sang from the hawthorn in my north-north-London garden. I didn't know what it was. But I was thrilled – thrilled beyond measure – to know that it was a bird I didn't know: thrilled to have isolated his song from a sea of songs I did know. This was progress; this was the beginning of being an insider. I pursued that bird hard: listening, trying to remember, and then looking it up on the tapes I now possessed. I made several false attempts: but then I had half an idea. I remembered sitting in Rob's garden after our day of censusing, eating a cheese sandwich and drinking a beer, while the same bird – the same species, anyway – sang endlessly, with a rambling, unstructured, rather inchoate delight in himself and in the season.

And I looked him up, and I had him: a garden warbler, a long-distance migrant, a late arriver, a song pretty enough if not exceptional, one I had no doubt heard without hearing on those stoned Burwalls dawns, and one which I was to hear, and triumphantly, not to say swankily, recognise in the Luangwa Valley on one of my many subsequent returns, thus very neatly completing the circle.

Oh, I was an insider now: a multi-sensed conjurer of birds from canopies. I liked to think I was a brilliant field man: I knew I was nothing of the kind. But then belonging is not a matter of expertise and knowledge. It's a matter of mind. I had walked and talked and listened with Bob and Jeremy and Rob: and as a result, I had changed my mind.

15. Lion
Panthera leo

Cowardice was something of a fashion. Wimpishness was cool. During my time at university, it was very much *à la mode* to boast about one's helplessness, one's neuroses, one's inability to cope with anything even remotely challenging or threatening. Perhaps there was a complex reverse snobbery in all this, and to do with drugs: if you couldn't cope with reality, it was because you were doing a lot of drugs. As the old joke had it, reality was a cop-out for people who couldn't handle drugs. Instead, you were intrepid in mental journeys. You were a dauntless traveller when it came to LSD: small surprise, then, that you lacked the psychic energy to cope with the washing-up, or that going to the supermarket was too heavy. Now I didn't wholly buy into this, and I was very quickly off the drugs bit, but I went along with the convention that difficult, dangerous, energetic things were not for the likes of us. We were all very amusing about this: certainly we amused ourselves.

This was not a line always slavishly followed. I had hitch-hiked to many adventures. One of the best of these began when Jim, my great friend from Burwalls, failed to keep his appointment with me in Florence. In the end, with colossal reluctance and with phantasmagorical wimpishness, I struck out on my own: and discovered, as the lone traveller always will, that adventures come far more easily and more frequently when there is no one else to get in the way.

But all the same, I returned from my travels and rejoined the culture of cowardice. Everything was too much and too heavy, from tutorials to cookery, from social events to human beings, from Pink Floyd to *Ulysses*, from one's own bank account to the global distribution of wealth. But of course, the biggest fear of all was scarcely, if ever, mentioned. What we dreaded above all things was the possibility – even, dear God, the inevitability – of entering the real world: of leaving the warm embrace of student life and taking up paid employment. We were paralysed with the fear that the best years of our life were almost over. We wanted to stay indoors, in the warm, knowing our friends would be dropping round any second, and that nothing we did would ever matter. One song haunted me: Bob Dylan's "Dream": "We thought we could sit forever in fun, But out chances really was a million to one."

Picture me, then, a couple of decades down the road. The Land Cruiser had taken me as far as it could: now I was standing on the banks of the Luangwa River, which was still swollen by rain. I was wearing khaki trousers, a shirt in bush green, on my head, a junglified hat, in my pocket, a knife. On my feet, nothing: socks rolled up inside my Timberland boots. I had bought these boots in New York, on the weekend after the Tyson-Holmes fight, when, reeling with flu, I had for some reason entered a shop and demanded the most expensive boots they possessed. I must have known, in my delirium, that a new phase of life was about to begin. Now the boots were worn-in and dusty. I tied them together by the laces and wrapped them carefully around my wrists, because I knew if I fell and lost them, I was buggered.

I am not sure to this day why Iain wanted me to wade the Luangwa River. Iain MacDonald was then running a safari operation in North Luangwa National Park, where there were no roads and no permanent camps. It is one of the world's wilder places. His camp was on an island on the edge of the park, and the river was too deep to cross by vehicle. There was a pontoon for bringing across heavy equipment, but Iain said that it would take too long to wait for them to get it ready. We should wade.

Now on my previous visit to the Luangwa Valley, I had observed the river, and as a result, I had seen crocodiles in extraordinary numbers and of extraordinary size. In the dry season, they could be found in groups of 100 or so, and up to 15 feet in length, some maybe even bigger, though I wasn't about to put a tape measure to them. On subsequent occasions, I was to see crocs taking large mammals. A baby elephant, for example. A croc, it seems, has two speeds, stop and light. They will lie without moving for days, immune to boredom, immune, it seems, to time itself; and then they will strike before you can begin to wonder if striking is an option.

So we waded. Iain led the way, while I recalled the theory that the leader is the safest: because he merely warns the crocs that others are on their way. It is the person who comes second that the crocs take. Me. The water was armpit deep and swift, and about 200 yards across. I held my boots high. Sergeant Wilson from *Dad's Army* whispered in my ear: "Do you think this is quite *wise?*"

It wasn't, to be frank. It was ever-so-slightly bloody stupid. I suspect that Iain was setting me a virility test: if I said too heavy and too much and I can't take it, or even is this wise, then I had failed and plans would be made accordingly. He had, after all, stressed the stressful nature of the trip when we met up in Lusaka. So I followed, splashing, swaying lightly and waving my boots about for balance, the water tugging at my trousers and playfully trying to unbutton my shirt, and the river got deeper and then it got shallower and in the end I was walking on dry land uneaten and in a glade of trees before a lagoon, and the lagoon was ringing with the triple whistle of white-faced duck and really, I was really rather in heaven. It was worth going through the crocs to get to this place. Or was the place just an excuse to go paddling with crocodiles? That was a dizzying thought, but I thrust it aside. We had more urgent matters to attend to. We had to find new camping places, a new marching route, and we had to get to the Mwaleshi River. And the Mwaleshi means one thing to old Luangwa hands. Lion.

Iain's safari operation was more than usually adventurous. You walked across the face of Africa, slept in a tent and lived right in the guts of the wilderness. But I wasn't on a proper safari with guests: this was a rigorous march to set up the operation for the new season. Now to be fair to myself, I had done a few reasonably intrepid things in my time, but all the same, this out-in-the-wilderness stuff was a step I had never considered. In normal circumstances, your life traces a continuous line from past to present: a process with at least some kind of logic. But this move from a horizontal, sofa-dwelling, fearful, life-is-too-heavy creature to someone who was about to walk across the face of Africa. This was not continuity but a violent rupture. This was not logic but contradiction. This was not an inevitable result of what had come before, but a violent, perhaps disastrous assertion of the will. Naturally, I was feeling a little wary. It was not just the question of whether I was physically up to the challenge: far more important was the question of whether I wanted to be there at all. Once out there – once committed – I might wish acutely to be somewhere else.

We all of us set off with some trepidation, then: me about whether or not the experience would be anything other than hideous, Iain about whether or not I would be a pain in the arse from beginning to end. He had told me about clients who had come with a wrong attitude, like the German who insisted on walking in motorbike gear to avoid the bites of tsetse flies. He collapsed with heat exhaustion on the first day.

So I set off in my bush gear, my binoculars in my hand, and off we marched. And marched. Now I had imagined that this would be much like the bush-walking I had already done: an easy stroll from one crowd of large mammals to the next. Instead, it was a rather dismaying revelation of African ecology. We saw nothing. Or very little. Eventually I understood why. If you walk close to the banks of the Luangwa River during the dry season, you see lots of animals because there is nowhere else for them to go. They have to drink, so they have to be in touch with the river. As the season moves towards its climax, the rush-hour crowds build up around the only water that can be had for miles, and the herbivores cling on while the carnivores make hay. This tension provides the best game-viewing in Africa.

But we walked not along the river but against the grain of the country, up and down and across, through large tracts of miombo woodlands: beautiful enough but all much the same and none of it exactly jumping with life. The spectacular gratifications of African travel were denied me. But I walked on, and I walked on, and I minded less and less. I began to feel something, not of the traditional African tourist's vision of the teeming of life, but of the African immensities, of the global remoteness. The only way on was walking: the only way back was walking. There was something oddly soothing in that thought. There wasn't much of an element of smugness in this either: get me, aren't I intrepid. No: there was a strange peace about it, a feeling that I had pushed my desires to be in the wild a fair old distance, and that I was still ready to keep going. This was not bravery. This was not even intrepidness. I was simply doing what I wanted to do and being where I wanted to be.

It was Africa that drove me on: the beauties, the vastnesses, the knowledge that whatever I saw, a great deal more saw me. A demented passion for the place slowly filled me: a wild, almost self-destructive love marked me for ever on that walk. At one stage we made a passage through ten-foot-high grass: the sort old Africa hands call adrenaline grass, because you can see nothing and you might walk into anything. And I was aware of the dangers, and aware of the excitements, but in a remote kind of way. I was, to be frank, filled with an insane joy at being where the big beasts were.

I remember one moment of revelation, when we came from the miombo and saw a vast open plain before us, full of short non-adrenaline grass and the animals that graze on it: impala, puku – a small toffee-coloured antelope that is something of a Luangwa speciality, zebra. There is something in such prospects that always catches at your heart: so many. It is a revelation of innocence, a revelation of a perfect world, a welcome to Eden. Of course you know that there might be lion or leopard under a bush and out of sight, but no matter: the sight of large numbers of large animals at peace with the world is something that goes very deep – well, humans first walked upright in plains just such as this; it is hard to think of anything that could possibly go deeper. We made a camp a short distance further on, for the river was, of course, close at hand. The next day we walked on.

Eventually, we reached the Mwaleshi, a tributary to the Luangwa that, unusually, flowed for most of the year. We camped there, ate as the sun went down and sat up in the growing dark while Iain told lion stories. Especially the one about the man who camped by this very river, perhaps in this very spot, or if not, scarcely a hundred yards away, and how he was taken by a lion, taken from his tent while

158

he slept, and devoured as sleep turned to waking and dream turned to reality. It was a lullaby. My profound and heartfelt response was to concentrate my mind on the urgent need not to get up and piss during the night. The vision of walking into a lion's mouth with nothing but my dick in my hand came to me with immense clarity. I found myself refusing water, tea, coffee. We had no beer: would I have refused that? I wasn't put to the test.

Around us, the lions began to wake. Now let us not think that a lion's call is anything like the petulant snarl you get before a Metro-Goldwin-Meyer film. A lion's roar is intended to be heard for miles. And in the Luangwa Valley, they use the rivers as amplifiers, as telephones, as channels of communication, and the roars fill the heavens. Not a single syllable, either, but a crescendo of coughing grunts impossibly loud, like a giant vomiting his heart out after the mother of all benders. This is followed by a pro-longed, huffing diminuendo. It often ends with a sigh: inaudible at distance. How close is a lion when you can hear the sigh? Old joke: too close.

I tried hard to piss every last drop from my bladder. And so to bed.

I had a tent to myself: flimsy, not sound-proof, not lion-proof. I stripped, clambered into my sleeping bag and prepared myself, not for slumber, but for the unfolding concert. I have never known a night like it for lion-music, neither before nor since. The Mwaleshi is one of the lion capitals of the world, and our unaccustomed incursion had stimulated them into song. And so one lion would call out: and a full pride chorus would answer. That is the best, or perhaps I mean the worst sound in the world: lion in the most ferocious numbers. I told myself, with impressive ethological understanding, that lions don't sing when they are hunting, because to do so would be counter-productive. You sing to other lions, and perhaps to humans, to point out that you are here and that this land is your land. When you hunt you do so in silence: you don't want to tell the buggers you are coming, after all. The lions were not hunting us: they were telling us about this part of the world and their place in it. And perhaps about our place in it.

Deafening, and all around, lion answered lion and pride answered pride and did so with heaven-splitting delight. It was as if they had found their voices for the first time: the first night of song in a world made new, one chance to raise their voices and they were going to get it absolutely right.

This trip to North Luangwa was the first time I had thought of myself as prey. This is quite different to being in a position of risk. It is not like the mischances and the perils you find as you knock about the world: the time when a car in which I had hitched a lift performed a 360-degree skid; the time a driver commenced a vigorous sexual assault on me at 60 mph; the midnight encounter with a gang in Port of Spain; the accidental small-hours hike up Eighth Avenue. This was not the same thing at all. I was not at risk of being injured or killed; I was at risk of being eaten. That is quite different from merely dying. The possibility puts the human being in a very different relationship to his environment from the one we normally accept. I was subservient to the landscape and to the big beasts that inhabited it. There were animals out there that saw me – at least to an extent – not as a source of threat but as a source of protein. I was not master of all I surveyed: I was merely part of the economy of the soil. Humans have been prey across the millennia: how ridiculous it is that we think of man-eating as an aberration, something that goes against the natural order. The exact opposite is true. It confirms the natural order, and our own place within it.

And I found that this experience had a potent savour: a profound resonance. I was not a unique and privileged thing, but part of the continuum of species. I was one with the impala and the puku and the zebra: we were brothers in edibility. I mean this in no fanciful way: we were all mammals together, and possessed broadly the same body-plan, and to a crocodile or a lion, there was not much difference, save that my Timberlands were probably more indigestible than hooves: and both should be left for the hyenas.

This sense – not so much of kinship as of oneness – was something I woke with, for I did manage some sleep on that cacophonous night. I got up, walked a certain distance from the camp, pissed long and gratefully and so returned to the human condition. But not entirely. Never again entirely. That sense of oneness, awakened by the night of music, was never to leave me. We walked back: and as I sipped at last a beer back in Iain's island camp, a bat hawk stole past at dusk.

16. Willow warbler
Phyolloscopus trochilus

My mother wanted me to be an international lawyer, a fact that tells us all kinds of interesting things about the relationship between fantasy and reality. She had lofty ambitions for me, and they cast a shadow over both our lives. These ambitions, as I knew from the time I took my eleven-plus, asked deep and searching questions about the nature of love: in particular, the extent to which love is conditional. These matters were not, perhaps, fully reconciled till the end.

I still turn my head away as the train pulls out of Barnes Station. I still stare down at my newspaper or my book, or out of the window on the opposite side of the tracks. I prefer not to look at the line of hedge that hides the path beyond, the path that leads to Putney Hospital. The

163

hospital has long been demolished, but that's not the point. To gaze on the path I took so many times, always with such craven thoughts in my head, is still too difficult. I prefer to keep my eyes elsewhere.

Education and subsequent high achievement was never my goal. Rather, it was my duty. My father, despite leaving school at 14, had become a high-up in the BBC, an oppressively hard act to follow. My mother had been unable to take up her place at Oxford because of the war, and this disappointment had marked her life. So I not only had to follow that tradition, I also had to make good the wrongs of the past. I was a vector for the ambitions of others, and my mother took on the job of keeping me from backsliding. A glorious future in international law was surely within my grasp.

But if these ambitions created tensions, they also created a kind of intimacy. There was a sense, when things were going well, of a conspiracy between my mother and me: against the rest of the family, against the rest of the world. We did it through books; we did it through scripture; we did it through narrative. There was something of a shared mindset.

My mother's considerable intelligence was her weapon, her stock-in-trade, her social persona. Tart, sometimes venomous one-liners gave her huge private delight. She meant no harm, or not much: but she could never resist the temptation of saying bad things. Mostly, this was the well-intentioned malice of gossip and complicity. But it was a dangerous game, and though highly adept at playing it, she was always capable of giving pain – especially to back-sliding sons.

Sherlock Holmes was a shared joy. By the age of 12, I had the Holmes canon more or less by heart: partly because I loved the tales, partly also because my mother loved them still more. Holmes gave us a language, it gave us a canonical text. We would play private games on long car journeys involving abstruse references to Holmes stories. We would concoct tabloid headlines, and the other person had to guess the story to which they referred. "Ancient riddle is crowning glory." "Too easy – *The Musgrave Ritual*."

The downside was the terrible bollockings, the shaming, accusing, horrendous tellings-off I received when my academic shortcomings were believed to have a basis in idleness, in insufficient ambition. When failure was of my own making, she was utterly unforgiving. This was ultimately to become counter-productive. As the 60s unfolded, it became an increasingly hard time for parents, particularly those seething with vicarious ambition. This was, after all, the first generation that had to learn that their sons and their daughters were beyond their command.

But even at the gaudy height of revolution, I still valued the literary conspiracy I had with my mother. She was a writer: I was an evolving writer. For a time, my literary tastes were skewed towards hers: I read Jane Austen, and though I realise now that I only sort of enjoyed the books – certainly I have never reread them – I valued them because a Jane conversation always put us on good terms. I read some of the other detective stories she loved: Josephine Tey, Michael Innes, Ngaio Marsh – but my enjoyment fell far short of unconditional love.

Besides, I was, treacherously, developing literary tastes of my own. I had violent crushes on TS Eliot and James Joyce, and so moved outside my mother's literary sphere. She was not an intellectual, not in the sense that loves analysis: but she had a profound sense of story. She wrote the *Blue Peter* historical pieces, and, with my father, co-wrote the *Blue Peter Special Assignments*. She had the knack of seeing history as a series of tales, and could bring that tale to life by finding a beginning, a middle and an end. A professional historian may curl his lip at such an approach: but stories are what humans love, and it is by stories that children – that all humans – most readily understand the world and the complexities of human life.

But me, I was forging in the smithy of my soul the uncreated conscience of my race, and the sweet Thames ran softly while I sang my song. Duty became a less pressing matter than literature, than fomenting revolution with Ralph, than fomenting still greater things with Christine, my lovely first girlfriend. I could feel the grasp of imposed ambition slipping, and that was intoxicating: but not as intoxicating as the rhythms and the wordplay of Joyce and Eliot. "He would create proudly out of the freedom and power of his soul... a living thing, new and soaring and beautiful, impalpable, imperishable." Not just him, I thought. Not just him.

Appropriateness. That was the key to my mother's soul, that was the secret of the universe. To say something was "suitable" was the highest form of praise. The idea of what was appropriate or suitable or fitting was what powered her religion, her view of society and her narrative technique. Good manners, right feeling, the Anglican faith – we sang "Firmly I believe and truly" at her mother's funeral, appropriately, and then, still more appropriately, at her own. The way that things fitted in, one with the other, bringing about a completion, a resolution, a meaning, was something that, in a quiet kind of way, enthralled her throughout her life. The right kind of thank-you letter, relations – she alone knew the difference between a second cousin and a first cousin once removed – the relationship between liturgy and scripture, the relationship between worldly life and a practical religion; all these were linked by a series of cosmic strands in her mind, making a glorious celestial map of connections and relationships. There is a moment in Anthony Burgess's *Earthly Powers*, when the narrator runs into Joyce in a café in Paris. "Joyce was drunk. He had an empty Sweet Afton packet in his hand, the cigarettes themselves lying on the ground virginal and wasted in a kind of quincunx pattern. Things tended to form into patterns for Joyce, but he could not see the fallen cigarettes at all…"

A quincunx pattern, by the way, is one like the five on a die. My mother would have liked this fact: she was always happy when in possession of privileged inform-ation. She would also have like the way I said die, correctly, rather than dice, which, being plural, is here incorrect. For things tended to form into patterns for her, too, though rather different patterns from Joyce's, and for that matter, mine. When she and my father had a mass said for their silver wedding, she chose the gospel, selecting the first miracle, the wedding at Cana in Galilee: the one in which they saved the best wine for the last. Suitable, you see. Appropriate. Very.

These patterns always linked us. Our conspiracy against the rest of the family, the rest of the world, continued almost in spite of ourselves. But I didn't make it to Oxford, falling at the fence of the Latin exam. It would have been appropriate if I had gone to Oxford, appropriate if I had righted the wrongs of her own life: my failure to do so was a disappointment on a cosmic scale. Her world view had failed her. Or I had. A cosmic thank-you letter had not been written. The connections had not been made.

There was to be consolation for her. When I was at school, I used to take *The Times* at half-price, a special offer, one designed to create a life-long loyalty. (Ha.)

Before long, she began to steal it from me each morning without shame. She began to identify with the paper: not the politics, but the ambience. The newspaper had a considerable sense of what was appropriate and what was not – and besides, the crossword soon became a daily confirmation of the cleverness of her mind, a confirmation of herself. I tried, for a while, to do the crossword myself, for the sake of our alliance, but it was a case of sorry, I can't manage it. For me, words were things that exploded with infinite possibilities: for her, words led to a single correct answer. It seemed that we had different ideas of what was appropriate.

But when, many years later, I began to write for *The Times*, it was a cosmic sign that things had not gone so badly wrong after all. Despite the difficult times on local papers, and the gloriously disreputable years in Asia, I was back in the world of appropriateness. It was a confirmation that things could work out well: that people could, in a phrase she always relished, "behave properly", even if they took their time about it. It was as if the universe itself had done her a favour – a favour it most certainly owed – by behaving properly. Would she have withheld her love, or some of it, if things had worked out differently, if I had behaved less properly, if I had failed to find professional success, if I had stayed in Asia writing novels? This was not put to the test, and as Aslan says in the Narnia stories – stories she always enjoyed for the serene patterns they drew with imagination and the Christian faith – no one is ever told *what would have happened*.

What did happen is that time passed and we all grew older, and my two sisters produced children and my mother was a grandmother and very pleased about it. She loved the large, noisy, bibulous family gatherings we had always gone in for, now with children underfoot adding to the hubbub; she was pleased that all her three children were in stable marriages and led interesting professional lives. She revelled in travel, though hated the turbulence travel brought with it. "We're off to Bali tomorrow and it's all absolutely ghastly," she once wrote to me on a postcard.

There were shadows in her life, no question about that. She grew overweight and was prone to tiredness; I suspect she suffered for most of her life from an undiagnosed thyroid problem. She also suffered from depression: "Churchill called it the Black Dog. But it isn't a dog. I like dogs. It's a Black Cloud." And often she sat in her black cloud, unable – as is the way with depression – even to try and escape its clutches.

She suffered a stroke in her late 60s, and it killed about half of her. She was told she would never walk again, but in a truly heroic effort, the last, she got back on her feet. We were optimistic that she would carry on much as before: it was not to be. Most of her joy in life was killed when the stroke hit her. She was no longer consistently clever: though there were still moments when the sharp-tongued picker-up of all references and nuances would suddenly appear in the conversation like a ghost.

I would visit her often, or quite often anyway, and frequently I would read from her favourite books, a recapitulation of the old alliance. She could still read well enough for herself, but it tired her to do so for long periods. Besides, the alliance gave pleasure to us both. But also we would talk, and two things bothered her: bothered her to the point of obsession. One question was whether her grandchildren would remember her only a sick old woman, rather than the acute person she had been when whole. I said they would always remember their gran who loved them: but that was no consolation at all. And the other question was worse: why? Why did she have a stroke? What had she done to deserve it? For her mind required that life should be tidied up and that even illness should be appropriate. And this wasn't. This wasn't appropriate, this wasn't suitable, this wasn't fair. "It's a biological caprice," I told her. "It's nothing to do with fairness. It's just fucking horrible luck." And she would shake her head and weep a little.

This shadow life continued for about three years. There were good bits, moments when she was cheerful, moments when her family racketed around her, glasses in their hands. But the bad bits lasted longer.

The second stroke killed her, but slowly, slowly. It was devastating: it took almost everything. It took the half-person that remained and reduced it to a tiny fragment of life, of spirit. I remember – one of those ineradicably vivid memories – the day she was moved to Putney Hospital, and the rest of us walked from the hospital out onto Barnes Common and then, for the first time that year, I heard the voice of willow warbler. Willow warbler: the sweet lisping celebrant of spring, the bird that tells you that the dark times are over, that the black clouds have dispersed, that the wait has been worthwhile. The willow warbler tells you that spring is no longer a promise but an achievement: that the time for the best of all that life offers is here, is now, is before us.

I had taken a sublime joy when I heard my first unilaterally identified first willow warbler of spring. That had been the previous year: the song expressed all my delight in spring, in wildlife, in my own growing familiarity with wild ways and wild things. Now, hearing the first willow warbler of the spring on Barnes Common, I didn't know what to think. Certainly I didn't take my cap from my head and hurl it into the air, as I had done the year before. And the bird, the song itself: was it a vindictive irony? Or was it, in the end, cosmically appropriate?

I visited the hospital often, or quite enough, and for the first few weeks, I heard the willow warblers singing every time: singing their ecstatic hymn to territory, to sex, to life; firmly, it seemed, they believed and truly. I would take the train to Barnes station and walk across the common, along the path that lay on the far side of the hedge. I would hope to find her asleep and so have to leave, and then feel dreadful shame at this fearful thought, and hope she was awake, but that she didn't want me to stay terribly long. At these times, our own pain, our own emotions, seek centre stage, and that is highly inappropriate. So I would find her and greet her, and talk and read to her: I kept a volume of *Palgrave's Golden Treasury* in my bag, because the words of the Victorians gave her some kind of peace. Some kind of pain, too, because she always wept. There was a sweetness about her at the end, something she never showed the world, perhaps never knew about herself. That was how I remember the last bit, the last visit: a sweet and mostly unfamiliar person.

So I left her for the last time, not knowing it was the last time, and Barnes Common stretched out before me; the willow warblers, now silent, were busy with the task of making more willow warblers. So did the willow warblers give me consolation, then? Did they help me to understand that despite everything, despite the bad, sad things that can be thrown at us, life goes on, and that the ineluctable forces of nature continue? Did they give me balance, perspective? Did they give me acceptance? Did they give me sanity? Did they give me a sense of cosmic appropriateness?

Did they fuck. Bloody birds.

17. Leopard
Panthera pardus

Manny Mvula was one of the first Zambians to pass his exams and become a guide in the South Luangwa National Park. At his oral, he gave a brilliant performance: easy, confident, quietly humorous, ironical, and above all, knowledgeable. One of the panel, white and an old Luangwa hand, asked him: "How did you come to know all this?" With a smile on his face and mischief in his heart, Manny answered politely: "I've read a lot of books."

I met Manny a few weeks after my mother's funeral. I was taking a two-month sabbatical, and spending it at Mchenja Bush Camp, thanks to the generosity of Savannah Trails, who were then operating the camp, and in particular, to Bob Stjernstedt, the Baron and birdsong guru I had met on my first trip to Africa. Cindy, with still greater generosity, had given her blessing to the trip,

For two months, my home was a hut on the banks of the Luangwa River, in a camp that lay at the opening of an ebony glade. I had a plan: I was going to write a wildlife book at the end of it, and I took pages of notes on all the marvels I saw. But I ended up writing a novel. If you spend a couple of months in the bush with the same people, you are going to establish an intriguing dynamic. There was Bob: the son of a Swedish baron and an English architect. There was Manny, the number two guide, and there was Jess, who had left England and ended up in the Luangwa Valley. She was 23, and she managed the catering with varying degrees of panache and panic. And me.

There were also two game scouts, uniformed men with ancient, battered rifles whose job was to keep us safe when we walked in the bush. Perry Nyama, tall and impossibly slim, was the cool one. I'd have faced a charging elephant with him. In fact, I did: we were close to a small group, me, Perry, Manny and a tough old girl of an English client, when a small female elephant got wind of us and gave us a bit of a charge. Perry, nonchalantly leaning on his rifle, merely let go of the weapon and gave a handclap; Manny did exactly the same thing at the same moment as the elephant got within, say, 20 yards. She turned and made off, as if embarrassed by her faux pas.

There was also the backroom staff. Fackson Banda, the cook, was a Friar Tuck figure who had constant rows with poor Jess; Derek Banda, a man with an extraordinarily soft voice, looked after the rooms and woke clients each day with a whispered good morning; Aubrey Njovu could fix absolutely anything and it was he who kept the whole Heath-Robinson organisation on the road.

I think it was my first night in camp that Bob nearly blew the place up. We had been discussing the voice of the wood owl, and the rhythm of its call. I suggested "now then – whooooo's a naughty boy?", but Bob had an alternative version. So he found his tape of wood owl and played it, and then we cranked up the volume and played it at the tree in the middle of camp to see if the resident wood owl was at home. He answered with cheery defiance, so Bob attached the spotlight to the batteries of the Land Cruiser and squirted at the tree until we had a fine view of this handsome owl. After that we went to bed.

The following morning, Aubrey noticed that there was a certain amount of smoke coming from the Land Cruiser. Bob had placed the spotlight face down on the seat, which was fair enough, but alas, he had forgotten to switch it off first. All night it had heated and smouldered and burned a deep hole into the seat: about the size and shape of a baked beans can. A mercy the thing hadn't taken light and set off the fuel tank – but Bob has the knack of lucky escapes. The first night of the season, he was showing Jess the constellations of the African sky when he stepped off the bank and plummeted ten feet below. Jess looked down at him starfished out on the bank. "I've only known him three hours and I've killed him already," she thought. But Bob scrambled to his feet, leaving a Bob-shaped hole in the mud, like a cartoon, and got on with running the camp, or trying to.

This was, then, something of a ramshackle operation. Mchenja was not classified as a lodge, but a bush camp. Its beauty came not from the luxury-in-the-wilderness thing but from the wilderness itself. Since I made my first visit there, it had made one small step upmarket, and one that I regretted. It now had concrete on the floors of the huts instead of river sand. But the rest was unchanged: my hut had two wobbly beds and a rickety table that bore a polite message asking couples not to entwine on the one bed. The showers were carved into living riverbank, and the lavatories were long-drops – that is to say, the seat was mounted over a deep hole. Fackson did the cooking on a fire and the baking in a tin in a hole beneath it. His bread, made fresh every morning, was a daily miracle. But then every day in the camp was a kind of miracle: one of long supply lines, insufficient money and insufficient clients, made good by people like Aubrey and Fackson.

There were tensions in the camp. Bob was a genius, but not everybody appreciated the fact. His charm, intelligence and knowledge generally overwhelmed the clients, but not all the African staff saw the point of him. Jess, as a first-season greenhorn, had to work hard to earn her respect; and Fackson, being an artist, was easily put out by innovation. "I am a *cook*," he would tell her, an absolutely unanswerable argument.

It was Manny who kept everybody working together smoothly. He would charm Italian clients in Italian, for he picked up languages with the enviable ease of an African. (Most Africans will speak two or three languages, for an African is the least insular person on earth: in fact, most of the people around the camp had picked up a smattering of Italian.) When Manny spoke in English, he could maintain an innuendo around the dinner table without for a second overstepping the mark of polite conversation, nor ever missing the point of the joke. He could talk with assurance of the ecology of the bush, confidently using recondite scientific terms. He knew all the scientific names of the trees, and also he knew all their medicinal properties, something he certainly didn't get from books. But also, at times when there were no clients in camp, he would disappear into the staff quarters and share *nshima* and relish: mealie-meal mixed with small amounts of meat and fish and veg, eaten with the hand from a common pot. He was as much at his ease there as he was anywhere else in the Luangwa Valley or, as things transpired, in the world.

Meanwhile, I was having one of the great times of my life. Denis's voice would wake me at 5.30 and I would wait until I had recognised ten birds on call before stirring: a process that normally took about 30 seconds. Then up for a walk: maybe with elephants and lions, maybe with ante-lopes and birds. Breakfast on return was followed by a shower and a nap. Then I would write up my notes. I had found some ancient staff-backed foolscap notebooks when I tidied my mother's study after the funeral, so I took them to Africa. I thought it was appropriate. They are filled with my italic scrawl: the unoriginal thought that Böhm's spine-tail looks more bat than bird; a mention of the duet of striped kingfishers, together with thoughts about why the valley has so many duettists; the urge, on seeing a pride of lion in affectionate corporate slumbers, to fling myself in among them and snuggle up. "To my surprise, everyone else in the vehicle chorused an agreement," I wrote of this incontinent confession. After lunch, I would sit by myself in the ebony glade till it was time to swallow a mug of tea and set off for the afternoon drive. We would stop, always at some appropriately beautiful place, for sundowners, for me always a bottle of Mosi, the local beer. After that we would drive through the night with the spotlight, looking for the night shift, quite different from the day shift: white-tailed mongoose and genet and honey badger. But always, we were seriously hunting for hunting leopards. Luangwa is the world capital for leopards. Find a leopard and we sent home happy clients: and most of the clients we sent home were pretty happy.

There was one evening when we had no clients at all. Manny proposed that we took the backroom staff out for a drive: there was enthusiastic agreement. So off we went, Manny at the wheel, Jess and I crammed tightly together – no hardship, at least not for me – in the front, and seven of the backroom boys wedged hip to hip in the back, not ideal for anyone except Fackson, whose build made for comfort in most circumstances. And so, with a great deal of giggling and shi-yiking, we set off. "*Attenzione alla testa*," Manny called as we passed beneath a low branch.

At once the game was on. Fackson began it, of course, a man with a huge appreciation for a jape. "*Perché?*" he called. "*Che terribile!* Bloody bad driver!"

At a stroke, they all decided to be querulous Italian clients. *Troppo veloce! Troppo lento! No me piace – voglio un leopardo!* Manny gave as good as he got. *Zitto! Zitto, eh! Maladetti italiani! Magari se avessi dei clienti simpatici africani!* We rolled on through the bush in holiday humour making a mighty din and laughing at the tops of our voices. But as soon as we reached Manny's favourite ebony glade there was an instant and perfect silence.

Leopard.

Is there anything more beautiful? Doubly beautiful in the dark picked out by the spotlight, the beam from our spot making him glow as if the light came from within. The perfect honey colour, with the immaculate maculations, the black rosettes. The long tail carried in a graceful arc, like an italic swash to complete this perfectly calligraphed beast. But the way he moved most of all: as if beneath the skin a gallon of oil lubricated every joint, making each movement preternaturally smooth, almost obscenely graceful. I never saw a pride of lions without wanting to join them: I never saw a leopard without wanting to be one.

And a leopard on business has his beauty tinged with the fizz of danger, with the fascination of narrative. What happens next? You have to find out, you must turn the page. The leopard flattened himself belly down, moving with sinuous wiggles towards the group of impala we could see resting up in the glade. Many of them: the more there are, the less likely it is to be you that gets eaten. There is safety in numbers all right: for all except one.

We stopped. Manny switched the engine off to create a voluptuous silence. We shone the light obliquely now, so that we didn't give away the leopard's position and spoil his hunt, so that we didn't dazzle the impala and make the hunt unfairly easy. We sat in a long silence, watching the dance of life and death take place before us: the endlessly patient stalk, the restlessness of the crowd of impala, who knew that something was amiss, but didn't know precisely what or where. They also knew that to break ranks and stand out from the crowd was suicide. Hold tight, then: and hope it's someone else that gets eaten tonight.

The silence was perfect and stayed perfect. No whispered conversations, no urgent requests, no shifting of positions despite our buttock-to-buttock seating arrangements. No real clients had ever held a comparable silence. And almost as imperceptibly as the growing of a plant, the leopard moved in: a process of terrible subtlety. It seemed as if this balance, this silence, this tension, would endure for ever.

And then the killing.

A silent charge, the explosion of alarm, the barks of horror, the crashing of undergrowth as a hundred impala fled, while one stayed behind, locked in the leopard's death-grip. The leopard's perfection was now marred by terrible panting: an explosion of effort such as this costs the leopard everything it has. The impala's perfection was for ever gone: its own grace a fading memory.

For most of our Italian clients, an animal is not an animal until it has been accorded an Italian adjective. Anything small or young: *ché carino*, how sweeeeet. A leopard: always *ché bello*, how beautiful. And a hyena was always ugly: *ché brutto*!

It was a hyena that now took over the drama, busting from the shadows of our vehicle – it must have been using us for cover – and cantering with a Halloween grin down to the hapless impala and the almost equally hapless leopard. The leopard fled at once: what else could he do? Fighting made no sense at all. A leopard must be perfect if he is to hunt, for a leopard hunts alone. An injured leopard is a hungry leopard, perhaps a dead one. His strategy is – must always be – to avoid confrontation. His strategy is perfection: and so he spun on his perfect haunches and vanished into the bush.

"Nooooooo!" Manny roared out his fury: the boys behind him shouted with the rage of disappointment. There was no joking now: Bastard! Bastard! And we charged him. Against all the rules of the park, we charged, bucketing downhill, everyone holding on with desperation, bashing and bruising each other, and the hyena looked up at this roaring, hollering, brightly lit dragon bearing down on him. He made the only possible decision. He fled too.

But not at once. Before doing so, he made a snatch at the impala with those nightmare jaws and ran off with something dangling from them. It was an unborn impala. The impala ewe was pregnant, and the hyena performed this lightning embryectomy to ensure that his evening had not been wasted. And then he too vanished.

Manny was awfully contrite afterwards. He knew the leopard would not come back and claim his own: he knew that the hyena, once we left, would be the one who came back and finished the lot. He knew that an anthropomorphic reading of natural events helps no one; after all, he had read a lot of books. He knew that the ecosystem operates in a way that works for hyenas and leopards and for that matter, impalas, and it will continue to work without our interference. But the horrible unfairness of the morality play of the bush had overwhelmed him as it had overwhelmed us all. We came back to the camp with a million contradictions in every mind.

I learned many things from my two months in the bush, not least that two months in the bush is as good a way of dealing with grief as exists anywhere on earth. I also learned, though perhaps I knew already, that wildlife, or indeed any kind of life, is not what you want it to be. Your own vision, your own hopes, are very inadequate instruments for understanding what is before you. Life is what it is, and it will carry on whether you agree with its principles or not. The meaning of life is life. Thus the hyena and the leopard and the impalas continued their interwoven lives, while I went back home, saddened and overjoyed.

Manny went on to become the most popular and successful guide in the valley. He travelled to England and the United States and elsewhere. He married an Englishwoman, and he now lives with her in Kent, returning to Africa periodically to manage his African affairs and get back to the wild. He has an MSc in tourism and conservation and he lectures in ecology, conservation, biodiversity and wildlife management. He and his wife Cheryl also run the High Five Club, a charity which operates poverty alleviation projects in Africa. Jess now manages Flat Dogs Camp in the valley with her husband Ade. Aubrey now works as a guide for another camp. Perry died of an AIDS-related illness. Bob runs Birding With Bob, specialising in avian adventures in Africa. Mchenja Camp still exists, though it has lost three metres of river frontage because of the relentless action of the Luangwa. It is very much smarter these days; the time of the long-drop has long passed. It is as beautiful as ever, and is run by Norman Carr Safaris.

18. Rabbit
Oryctolagus cuniculus

He couldn't walk, but he could trundle all right. Never a great one for crawling, he got the hang of the trundler as soon as he could stand, the trundler being the usual sort of brick-barrow, with a handle that was shoulder high, at least for him. He could lean on that and step out precariously across the carpet. Naturally, there were a few falls – and it's a nasty thing to fall on – but he was soon more upright than not. And the weather was beginning to get better, and every now and then he would essay a trundle about the garden, so of course, our thoughts turned to adventure.

Joe was coming up to one, and was a great adventure in himself. Rum thing, parenthood: you spend all those months worrying about it – and that moment when you go home with a baby for the first time is the single most ter-rifying thing that ever happens to anybody – but once your bluff has been called, it's as if it's always been like that: as if you'd always been three and not two.

Many of my friends declared that having children wouldn't change their lives. They more or less instantly discovered that you might as well say that death won't change your life. Everything is changed. I remember the first evening when Cind and I dared to leave Joe in the hands of Cind's mother for a couple of hours: we went to Pizza Express and talked about Joe. Well, what else was relevant?

He got bigger, as they tend to. He stopped lying about and started rolling. After that, he did marine iguana imper-sonations: holding himself up on two straight arms. Then he stood against chairs and tables, and soon, he began to crawl and then almost instantly, to trundle. So Joe and I went on an adventure, not our last: and this particular adventure became a daily ritual for what seems like an age. It can only have been a few weeks.

We trundled out of the garden, through the back gate that opened onto the little wood, and along the broad path. Then we turned left, on the path that led along the railway track to the station; as I have said, our house was built on the roof of a railway tunnel. We went as far as the place where the view opened out, a considerable distance to trundle, especially for someone who couldn't actually walk: a couple of hundred yards. But it was worth doing, because it was a place of enchantment.

We could look down and see wonders. We could see trains; we could see rabbits. The trains went past every few minutes: expresses from King's Cross going to Yorkshire and Newcastle and Scotland; suburban trains to Stevenage and Cambridge; the local ones that went as far as Welwyn Garden City. We waved to the trains, identifying each of the three species as they passed. And we also watched the rabbits.

The path was at the top of the cutting that led to the southern entrance of the tunnel, and the rabbits lived on the slope of the cutting. The precipitous sward was kept short by their constant grazing, and at that time of day, for it was always early evening when we trundled, the rabbits were at their best: grazing contentedly, and going hoppity-hop with a nonchalance that suggested they'd never seen a fox in their lives. Behind their fence, on that slope, they were even safe from most dogs. These were rabbits of privilege. They positively flaunted themselves for our pleasure, while the trains rattled and gave out their wails in a minor third. Frseeeeeeeefronnng! That was Molly Bloom's train whistle, but it'll do for the cries of trains entering and leaving our tunnel, with the bunnies never cocking an ear nor twitching a hind leg nor flashing a scut.

Was it the trains that gave Joe such delight, or the

bunnies? Or the journey itself? It was all three, of course, and both of us swept up in the extraordinary business of journeys and life and experience: me, and the small me that wasn't me at all.

Bunnies and birdies and choochoo trains: they're all part of growing up. The way we first come to terms with our own life is by contemplating other lives. The realisation that there are non-human creatures in the world – like us, but not us – is not just a pretty decoration in the child's book: it is the portal of understanding and the beginning of language. A child may not be able to talk: but ask what a cow says and a sheep says and a doggy says and a cat says, and speech has begun. Moooo! In the Babel of the farmyards and jungles of the nursery we learn speech and we learn about life's possibilities: with baa and woof and meow and quack our consciousness is formed. Non-human life fascinates: enthrals: non-human life is the great adventure of childhood.

We would turn and go back home. Joe, now righteously tired from his exertions and from the wildness of the adventure, would sit in the trundler with his knees up round his ears, and I would trundle us back up the railway path through the wood, through the back gate, across the garden and back into the kitchen.

I remember reading a book review in, I think, the *Spectator*, in which the reviewer comes across a passage in a biography or memoir, in which the author or subject says with vague regret that he had never "seen" his son "being bathed". The reviewer added that on reading this, he realised for the first time that he had never "witnessed that ceremony" himself. It was one of those moments when you feel profoundly thankful that you live in the age that you do: when you can, for once, praise modernity and advancement and change rather than regret the errors of past generations. For a modern father, the idea of "witnessing", still less not witnessing the ceremony, are almost equally unthinkable. A modern father conducts the ceremony: plays splashing games, persecutes with the Demon Boy Squirter, sinks the ducks and the boats, and does the stuff afterwards with towels and nappies and sleep-suits. It is required behaviour for us all and everyone involved – mother, father, child – is the richer because of it.

I don't want to overstate my claims for hands-on parenting, not least because Cind will read these words at some stage. But I did my bit, or some of it. So on some nights I would put Joe to bed and read him a story. And yes, it generally had animals in it, not because I had chosen it but because he had.

David Attenborough is often asked how he got his love of animals. His response is to ask: "How did you ever lose yours?" Every child loves and is fascinated by animals. I did, I was. The difference is that many people lose that fascination: I can speak here with immense authority, because I did myself. I was lucky: it was there under the

190

surface all along, bubbling away, crying out for release.

In teenage years we seek symbols and badges of maturity: clothes, haircuts, records, cigarettes, beers. We reject things that might make us seem immature: public displays of parental affection, religion, the things we liked when we were younger. One of the things we reject is the wild world: God forbid that anyone should think us soppy about furry animals. Oddly, we don't reject childhood games. Football, a child's game frequently loved by children, seamlessly becomes a passion in youth and maturity. But the wild world – not childish at all – is regarded as a childish thing and to be put aside as quickly as possible.

Picasso said that it took him four years to paint like Raphael and a lifetime to paint like a child. My loss of the wild world was one of the great errors of my life: the slow regaining of that love and the beginning of an understanding – the realisation that this is not a childish thing at all – has been one of the great joys of my life. All the same, I don't think it is true that to find something you must first lose it. Every child finds the wild world, at least by means of the imagination. I don't think that losing it makes you understand its value still more, either: I know many people, starting with Attenborough, whose love has never wavered, still less weakened.

I didn't want Joe to lose it either. But what can a parent do? You want so many things for a child. I wanted Joe to become a kind of super-me: perhaps a great ethologist and writer, the Konrad Lorenz of the new millennium. But one of the wonders of those very first few months is the realisation that you have a complete personality already there: that everything that happens is consistent with what happened before. This understanding comes to a parent long before crawling and walking is an option. I'd find it hard to say what that personality was – hard enough to find the right words even for a fully made personality – but it's one of the things that strikes every parent with wonder and yet, at the same time, is quite blindingly obvious.

It is a universal experience of parenthood: there is a part of you that wants to make a mark, to shape and forge and mould, but you realise almost from the beginning that you can do nothing of the kind. Part of me wanted, and wants to make sure that Joe is long-haired, word-drunk, with addictive reading habits, a great naturalist, finding when the time is ripe a taste for cold beer and malt whisky, heterosexual, monogamous, a person who loves to discuss wildlife and sport and *Ulysses*, a horseman, a person with a taste for abstract ideas, and first and most importantly, a writer. But Joe isn't going to turn into a super-me, and never looked like doing so. All a parent can do is open doors and be there with any kind of assistance and support and encouragement that may be necessary: or, to be brief and economical with my words, to be utterly and brutally frank, offer love, uncritical and unconditional. I had failed to be an international lawyer: Joe is not going to be any of the things that I might have planned for him. That is parenthood almost from the beginning: it means that you might as well stop making plans. This third person is not you. It is not even half you, as an elementary reading of genetics would suggest. He is completely and hermetically himself: he may have half his genes from each of his parents, but the mixture is unique, and the way he develops and comes to understand the world is beyond all control.

Parenthood is not an abandonment of responsibility: it is the exact opposite. But it is not something you get on your own terms. You have responsibility without power. You can oppress and bully and push, as some parents do, but you can't create a personality because it's already there. Perhaps you can destroy one: but that's not something many of us want to investigate.

We trundled up and down that path as spring arrived, and I told Joe about the birds that sang and the plants that flowered. And soon Joe no longer needed the trundler to stay upright, but he took it anyway, for the security and for the love of ritual and for the pleasure of the ride home. We would identify the three species of train, and watch the rabbits at their evening graze, great fat contented things, living within touching distance of the crazy and destructive world that humans have created, and yet somehow immune from it: safe in a land of plenty, a fence to keep out danger, and no ambition but to stay in it for ever. All I wanted was to create a country like that for my son: but that, like the son himself, was beyond my control. We turned for home: Joe in the brick-bed of the trundler, knees up round his ears, and me bent in half as I pushed him back up the hill.

19. Sea otter
Enhydra lutris

The art of travel is the art of sanity. It's an exercise in clinging onto your soul in the face of mighty opposition. It is not easy: mostly because people who do a lot of travelling tend to be, to a greater or lesser extent, neurotic. You have to be slightly nuts or the constant changes of the travelling life would have no appeal: on the other hand, if you start out slightly nuts, the job of keeping sane is all the more challenging. You have to master logistics, and you have to master personal comfort.

Each traveller has his own method, tested over time until it becomes a matter of curious pride. The methodology of travel is an extension of the self, an expression, at least ostensibly, of all the better parts of one's personality. And unfortunately for everybody else, it is something most travellers talk about ad nauseam.

Oh yes, always get the last flight of the day out of JFK, and before getting the cab, have an early supper; I always used that place opposite the Lincoln Center. I would check in, requesting an aisle seat, and then consume two Wild Turkeys on the rocks in the bar. Once on the plane, I would pull a hoarded sleep-mask from my pocket and, refusing all food and drink, attempt to sleep until we were told to stow our tray tables and place our seatbacks in the upright position. I could give you a great deal more detail, in the unlikely event that this were of the slightest interest, most of it designed to tell you how fabulous I am and how provincial and inadequate most other people are in comparison. For I was, for a while, fairly utterly fabulous: a *Times*-lord, a *Times*-traveller exploring the far reaches of sporting space and time for my newspaper, jaywalking at my ease across the stratosphere.

So I had a special place for my travel documents, and another for my wallet with credit cards, and still another for the accreditation I needed to get into the sporting events. And I would have my carry-on baggage meticulously filled with things that could not be trusted to the hold (laptop, binoculars, latterly phone charger) plus journey comforts (books, Walkman, tapes, latterly iPod) and on and on and on.

Then to the hotel. You must establish some kind of claim over your room, somehow plaster your name over its anonymity. If I was staying more than a couple of days, I would always unpack a few things: certainly the books, for I always travel with an inordinate number. Thus I would cruise about the sporting world, the Goldberg Variations on the headphones, a guidebook to the places I was visiting and a raft of heavyweight literature which I read even when people weren't looking, all the time worrying about departure times and connections and reservations and taxis and deadlines and the question of being able to write anything at all.

And there would be great days and there would be OK days and there would be days of nightmare: all of them coming in that exaggeratedly high relief that comes with being away from home. And I loved it: I loved the adventure, I loved the self-importance, I loved the sport, I loved the writing. But increasingly, that wasn't enough: because I also loved the birding.

The books were always the heaviest part of my baggage, and I would always take a bird book, sometimes two if I were travelling, say, to the eastern and to the western United States. I remember visiting Foyle's before my first long-haul sporting trip, and buying for a wince-making £25 *A Guide to the Birds of Trinidad and Tobago* by the majestically named Richard ffrench. I went to Trinidad to write the final chapter of a biography of the England cricketer, Phil Edmonds, and to write some pieces for *The Times*. The publishers bought the plane ticket, the rest I found myself.

The year was 1986; the West Indies team were both dominant and ruthless; the England team were in disarray and on their way to a 5-0 defeat in the series: a blackwash. I reported fragments of this story with some enthusiasm, while the *Times* cricket correspondent, John Woodcock, gave his own measured censure. And no matter how hard we tried, everything kept coming back to the extraordinary Ian Botham: brilliant, inspired, impetuous, a man with no self-critical faculties whatsoever, raucous, pig-headed, a strident alpha male with a taste for assembling a court of admirers around himself, a hugely likeable man when he turned on the charm, as I was to discover later, but also a man to beware of, always a man with a hint of danger about him.

In those quaint old days, the press and the players stayed in the same hotel. (Not me: I was staying in a guest house up in the hills of Malabar.) Journos and players would mingle amicably in the bar of an evening, in a manner unthinkable today. But Botham was never among them. He was the first cricketer to attract the tabloid news hounds on a regular basis, and he decided that the best way to avoid trouble was to lurk in his room with a few chosen companions. This self-incarceration was torment to him, and it didn't work, either, for he found scandal in the next leg of the tour when the team went to Barbados. (As a point of information, Botham always denied that anything untoward took place between himself and Miss Barbados, and says that the story that they broke a bed together is untrue.) He was a man oppressed and unhappy, out of sorts with himself and out of touch with his game. At the second Test of the series, played in Port of Spain, Trinidad, Botham made two in the first innings, one in the second. He was out at the moment when England looked as if they might just make a decent fist of things. It was a blow from which England never recovered, in the match and in the series. Botham knew he would be condemned for his failure, and as he walked off the pitch, he turned towards the press box and made a mime of a man suspending himself from a noose. Go on then, you bastards, hang me. It was the big story of the day: of the match.

A news cameraman caught this exit on camera and then had the wit to pan towards the press box to capture the stony faces of his judges, all turned solemnly and sadly towards the failed hero. The film was shown on the national news back in Britain, and the nation observed that one journalist was not gazing at Botham. Alas, the camera clearly showed someone hanging out of the press box with binoculars trained on something at 90 degrees to the action. I even remember what bird it was: a crested oropendola. You can see it on the cover of the old editions of Ffrench's book: a chunky black thing with a blazing comet-tail of yellow.

In that moment, I was skewered for ever, caught

exactly as I am for all time: a man stuck between two worlds. Just like the human race, really: one half wrapped up in the affairs of humankind, the other half swept into the wilder world beyond. As a writer, too, I was neatly sliced in half in that instant, as if by a magician: Botham holding one end of the saw and the oropendola the other.

The oropendola set a pattern, and I have followed it throughout my professional life. I would watch sport with delight, but with my eyes constantly escaping, attracted to a movement in the sky. I like to think that my involvement in two wildly different worlds has been an advantage, each side informing the other, taking away the strait and blinkered vision of the specialist. But I wonder also if my life as a professional writer has not been fatally split: perhaps a too-wide fascination with too many different things has compromised any ability I might have.

These thrilling but slightly ludicrous collisions between the sporting life and the wild have happened all over the world, and I have always treasured them. I have a long shelf of field guides, comparatively few of them bought for purpose-built wildlife trips. Instead, I have lugged them around in the hope of chance encounters in the midst of all those sporting journeys, in search of moments that would lift the day beyond the human and the humdrum. I remember receiving not one but two phone calls during the football World Cup of 1994 in the United States, after a match at the Rose Bowl in Pasadena: both from colleagues on other papers wanting to know what bird it was that had flown so ominously across the stadium with a dead lizard in its claws. I was delighted to tell them it was a red-tailed hawk: disappointing them, I suspect, because they wanted it to be a vulture or an eagle, for this was a match fraught with significance. Colombia, pre-tournament favourites, were eliminated after their match against the United States, in which it seemed Colombia didn't try a yard. Pablo Escobar scored an own goal and was assassinated when he got home to Medellin. An augury is, by etymology, a truth revealed by the behaviour of birds.

But more often, the encounters with birds and other forms of wildlife have been pleasingly random. I have always savoured birds that entered the stadium and became participants in the drama: a shikra at the Wankhede Stadium in Bombay; a lesser kestrel at the Stadium of Light in Lisbon; alpine swift over the Olympic complex in Athens; red-rumped swallow in the Bird's Nest Stadium in Beijing.

Whenever possible, I would seek relief from the intensity of travel, the pressure of work and the thrilling self-regard of sport, of humankind and of myself, and play truant. I would cease to be a swaggering hard-travellin' professional sportswriter and become a birder: a nerd, in the eyes of all save myself. I would enter the phone box and willingly emerge as Clark Kent. And so I found roseate spoonbill near a rubbish incinerator in Florida, New

World warblers in Central Park, cinnamon teal in LA.

My New York rituals changed. For some years, I had a dizzying if one-sided love affair with New York: oh yes, ten minutes in the place and I was a tough-talking New Yorker myself. I knew special places to eat and drink, remarkable places to buy stuff, fabulous places to walk and hang out. New York became a kind of Venice to me, an impossible, magical and utterly romantic place in which exoticisms could be found at every step. The enthralling bookshops seldom saw me pass them by, and I bought a many books about the wild world: Gould, Singer, Moss, Schaller, Ridley, Tudge, de Waal, Wilson.

But in the midst of this love affair, I found an intoxication beyond the 50-block strolls down Fifth Avenue, the hanging-out in East Village, the pavement beers as I watched New York's endless parade of the gorgeous and the mad. I found an escape: one which both nullified the city and made it still more wonderful. I would get the subway. I would take the clanking A train away from Manhattan, away from my hotel on Central Park West, fancying myself no end of an intercontinental adventurer as I did so, a train going either to Rockaway Park or Far Rockaway, wonderful romantic destinations, but I would get off before the line split, at the more prosaically named Broad Channel, and walk through an utterly changed landscape of wind-blasted wooden houses with plastic bags rolling down the street like tumbleweed, a lost sad place in which you constantly expected to meet Kurt Vonnegut heroes selling storm windows.

The big sky was filled with planes, for this was almost beneath the flight path of JFK. I would walk briskly through these streets, as far, it seemed, from downtown Manhattan as the moon, and make my way to Jamaica Bay Wildlife Refuge, and there I would see birds: the more beautiful, the more remarkable, for their proximity to the city. The refuge covers getting on for 10,000 acres, and more than 300 species have been seen there: and I saw plenty on various visits in various seasons: redstarts, willets, night herons, egrets, scaups.

But I remember it best on a wild winter's day when the wind whistled through the canyons of Manhattan, and leaving the bars, or even my hotel room, seemed an act of folly. But acts of folly have always been something I am good at, and so I walked, trained, walked: and then stumped around the refuge, collar of my townie coat around my ears, relishing the birds, the scenery, the big sky, my own bravery, my own folly. And then, just to reward me, just as I was turning to leave, the dusk came and birds began to fall from the sky: big white birds with black-tipped wings. The snow geese were coming: and my heart rejoiced: bird after bird after bird, a wild world with the most citified city of them all just a train ride away. My crazily split professional life seemed validated in that long moment as the fine plump birds descended in their fine fat numbers.

Other days, other journeys, other truancies. Ground hornbills on a lightning trip to the Masai Mara, when I had been in Nairobi writing about Kenyan runners. Black kites over a Zen temple in Japan during the World Cup of 2002. Painted stork in a trip to Bharatpur during a cricket tournament. Great crested grebes, seen during a break in the cricket at Nottingham. During the Olympic Games of 2008, I even wrote my weekly wildlife column from Beijing. In the three and a half weeks I compiled a list of 13 birds, later amended to 12; I decided later that the barn swallows I claimed were all red-rumped. Even here, even amidst the enthralling craziness and the glorious wall-to-wall 16-hours-a-day action of the Olympic Games, I found the odd moment to look skywards. The sky was mostly filled with smog and dragonflies and those red-rumped swallows, but on two occasions I saw a falcon: a hobby, a dashing and thrilling killer that eats both dragonflies and swallows.

I have been known to push these things too far. Like the time I was covering Nigel Mansell's first taste of motor-racing in the United States in 1993. He was testing at Laguna Seca raceway in Monterrey, California, and I watched him in the morning, did the press conference and got the story, and then, while he was at it again in the afternoon, I slipped off to walk along the seafront. The sea lions barked and plunged, but I was looking for something else. I found it when I found the right bar. It was at the end of a pier, and I sat there drinking Mexican beer and gazing out at the kelp-beds: and there they were, sea otters swimming and playing and feeding, so lovely that I longed to swim out into the ocean and join them. I peered through my binoculars, pausing occasionally to order another beer, while the sea otters lay on their backs in the water, cracking abalone shells with stones on their tums in the time-honoured sea otter way. And they were glorious and the world was ditto, and I had another beer, and said to myself: this is fine. This is wonderful. This is perfect. And to think you are being paid to do this!

It was with a douche of horror that I remembered I was in fact being paid to write about Mansell, and I needed to file copy within two hours. A further douche: what if he had killed himself in afternoon practice and I never knew? This would have been the ultimate journalistic cock-up. I ran incontinently back to my hotel and rang Mansell's fixer, for this was in the time before mobile phones. I got through first time and was told that Mansell had set a new lap record for Laguna Seca and gone home happy, saying nothing more. And so I wrote my story and filed it, my mind occasionally flitting back to those fabulous fat sinuous beasts that plied their trade among the long strands of kelp: the furriest animal on the planet, for the thickness of their coats wards off the ocean chills. I had, I knew, stolen something. I had stolen a fragment of wild from the routine of the tame. Pausing only to acknowledge to God that I owed Him one, I hammered out a really fairly decent tale, in content if not in style. I was told that I had done well: just how well, I kept to myself.

20. Tiger
Panthera tigris

For some years I shared my house with a tiger. Well, he was only intermittently a tiger, but the times when he was a tiger were profoundly significant for us both. I remember the first time: he was at his grandmother's house and came across a tiger mask. Not precisely a mask: it was more like a hold-the-front-page green eyeshade, but with tiger stripes on the peak and a superstructure that included tigrine eyes and ears. It was a mask, then, without the claustrophobia of masks, and Eddie regarded it gravely for some time. When I helped him put it on, as much for my own amusement as his, the transformation, the transfiguration took place. Eddie roared. He made his fingers into claws and roared again. After that, for once Eddie has taken a fancy to a notion he is reluctant to let it go, he spent a great deal of the evening roaring and it seemed likely that we would need to get the tiger mask surgically removed before he went to bed.

Eddie is my second son, and he has Down's syndrome. Animals have been as important in his growing up as they have been for Joe, as they are for every developing human. The signing system of Makaton has been of immense importance to him, and among the first signs he was able to do (after biscuit) were cat and dog. To sign cat, you draw whiskers on your face with your finger-tips, to sign dog, you stab downwards, paw-like, with two fingers on each hand.

Our dog Gabriel, a black Labrador bitch, helped shape Eddie's universe. A deep joy in Eddie's life was to curl up alongside her in her basket. If ever Gabriel causes me passing irritation, I remind myself that she is not so much an angel as a saint, whose generosity to Eddie is worth commemorating on a stained-glass window. She has scarcely uttered a cross word in Eddie's direction, never once snapped: only occasionally, when the ear-pulling and tail-tugging became too oppressive, she would sigh and walk into another room. Because of Gabe, Eddie knew he was living in a world full of kind and generous creatures.

I was rung up the other day by someone I had never met. His wife had just given birth to a girl with Down's, and he was struggling. So I was happy to talk about my own experience: to tell him that, really, it's not something to get too desperate about. It seldom occurs to me that Eddie's life could have been something else: I have never for an instant thought that our family is blighted or even compromised by his existence. The exact opposite is true. Nor am I an angel or a saint: I am just another dad, getting on with things as best he can, trying to emphasise love above exasperation.

We had been told after the scans that there was a 50 per cent chance that he would have Down's. We didn't go for an amniocentesis, because that might have killed him, and in any case, Cind was not considering a termination: not her way, to evade responsibility for anyone or anything put in her charge. Long before he was born, or before Cind knew of his nature or his condition, Eddie was the beneficiary of the most ferocious love: of a loyalty without question or constraint. That's Cind's way. Me, I followed, a poor but enthusiastic second. So Eddie was born and had two holes in his heart, and our immediate concern was not the nature or the fact of his Down's syndrome but whether or not he would live. He had open-heart surgery at four months, and now, aged eight, he is built like a little bull.

But it was as a tiger that I knew him in his early years, for his imagination was unreservedly caught by two books. His understanding has always been much greater than his ability to speak. It is hard for him to make words physically, hence the massive importance of the signs. It is not always obvious how much he has understood of any situation or story; the answer always turns out to be slightly more than I assumed.

Like all children, he loved and loves books and stories, and like all children, he loves them particularly when there are animals. Animals were for him, as they are for everyone else, the key to language and the gateway to the imagination. And so, for many nights, every time when it was me that did the putting-to-bed ritual, we read one or other of the tiger books.

The first was *The Loudest Roar*, by Thomas Taylor, and it is about Clovis. Clovis is a small tiger with an enormous roar, and he lurks about in a jungle full of all kinds of unexpected creatures – Taylor is not pedantic about zoo geography – and he sneaks up on them and he goes – well, I think you can work out what the roaringest tiger always does. But here was a book that Eddie not only enjoyed but also participated in: he too roared. He was Clovis, lurking in the thickets and forests of the blankets and leaping out on unsuspecting hippos and wildebeest and macaws to roar. And it was a special delight for me that Eddie joined in, was fully up to speed with the doings of Clovis. In the end, all the animals gang up and roar at Clovis, and he becomes a much better tiger for ever afterwards... but every night, he regressed and started his programme of lurking and roaring again, and Eddie was Clovis once more and he roared his way towards sleep every night.

The other tiger book was even better. This was Judith Kerr's masterpiece, *The Tiger Who Came to Tea*. Kerr fled from Germany at the age of ten in 1933 with her Jewish family and settled in Britain. She wrote the 17 Mog books, but none of them can touch *The Tiger*, first published in 1968. Sophie and her mummy are sitting down for tea when there is a ring at the doorbell. Sophie's mummy opens the door and it's a tiger. "Excuse me, but I'm very hungry. Do you think I could come in and have some tea with you?" Of course!

The tiger is offered a sandwich, but he doesn't take just one sandwich. He eats all the sandwiches on the plate! Step by step, he eats everything in the house, and drinks everything too, including Daddy's beer. Then he says: "Thank you for my nice tea. I think I'd better go now." The pictures show the tiger huge, sensuous, wicked, but not unkind. Sophie is fascinated, always as close to the tiger as she can be as he licks out the saucepans and cleans outs the cupboards. It is the most glorious image of the wild world coming to visit the safe and settled and citified: wildlife intersecting mysteriously with tamelife – which is, of course, exactly what I am trying to do with this book, or perhaps I mean with this life.

Joe had also adored *The Tiger* in his time. He was, of course, younger than Eddie when he first encountered it. He was so much in awe of the book, its subject and its themes that he never spoke of the tiger at all. When he wanted the book read, he asked always for "Sophie". The tiger was too deep, too mysterious, too awe-inspiring, too important for casual mention. Eddie's love for the tiger was different from the almost religious feelings that Joe held for it: but it was the same silent fascination, the same glorious respect for the wild possibilities that were inherent in the book, in the kitchen, at the tea table. The tiger was a member of our household.

So when it came to National Book Day, and all the children had to dress up as their favourite literary characters, there was no questioning the matter. Eddie goes to a village school in Suffolk, where he is much cherished and has tremendous support. We got him a tiger costume, and he was so delighted he couldn't speak. Then came the day in which he was to go to school as a tiger, as the Tiger – but alas, he went down with a cold. A cold is a hard thing for a child with Down's, because their tubes are extremely narrow. Breathing is difficult even at the best of times; a cold robs Eddie of sleep and of comfort, for he can't suck his thumb, and it casts him down, utterly. He was deeply dispirited, but determined to go to school as a tiger: a very sad, tearful, snotty, red-nosed tiger he was too. He threw up in his tiger-suit and he had to come home before the day was done. Eddie the sad tiger was a heartbreaking sight: it had all started so well and ended so poorly. Eddie lacked the philosophical basis to give these things the perspective most children his age possess. It was a bitter blow.

But the following year, the two tiger books were still part of our lives, and the Tiger, the one who ate the cakes and drank the tea from the teapot and drank all the water in the tap, was still Eddie's favourite book. And so he went to school in his stripes once again, this time as a happy tiger. So the story, like all the best stories, has a happy ending.

What's Eddie for? A question worth asking, I think. The Nazis sent people with Down's to the ovens, because they polluted the purity of the race. And before we shudder at such barbarity, we should remember that most women pregnant with a child with Down's syndrome choose to abort. It's clear that many people believe that a child with Down's has no point: that such a being is extraneous to human needs, a mere burden on society and in particular, on the parents. Best get rid of them.

The reality of Eddie's life contradicts all of that. At school, he is held very dear. The headmistress has said that her school is a better place for his presence: because Eddie is there, the school's small society has become more caring, more gentle, more at ease with itself. At the end of the last school year, Eddie won the Peace Prize, voted for annually by the entire class. The prize is given to the kindest, most generous and most helpful child.

Eddie comes with us to shops and restaurants and pubs and cafés, and I have never heard a whisper of distaste. *Au contraire*: Eddie, when in a sunny mood, becomes an instant favourite, the people he encounters relishing the chance to do small things to make him happy.

Is that enough, though? Shouldn't an individual contribute something to society? Eddie's function is to be loved, and to love in return. Perhaps that is everybody's ultimate function. Eddie enriches the lives of his family and enriches the lives of those he comes into contact with outside. That seems to me to be a life right on the cutting-edge of usefulness.

It's some time now since Eddie was last a tiger. He is often a dog, and will fetch sticks and bark; and he is sometimes a cat. His current favourite book is about a dog called Floppy who rescues a litter of puppies from a fire, part of an inspiring series with which he is learning to read. He does, however, still sometimes give a jocular roar when it seems appropriate. Once a tiger, always a tiger.

21. Morelet's crocodile
Crocodylus moreleti

The first thing you need when putting together an expedition to the rainforest is the right company. You want people who love wildlife, are prepared to put up with discomfort, are unfazed by things like remoteness and wildness and lack of room service and what would happen if you got appendicitis, who do not have a problem with the fact that there is absolutely nothing to do except look at wildlife (and in the rainforest, you don't often see very much of it), who will not be overly twitchy about the possibility of snakes and can cope with the omnipresent actuality of invertebrate life. So here's what we came up with: one PR person from Jaguar, one very small female Greek fashion photographer, one very large male Canadian make-up artist, a celeb journo ("I'm not a celebrity journalist; I mainly write about alternative therapies"), an obsessive birder with a passion for digi-scoping, and me. Oh, and a film star. Darryl Hannah came with us to Belize. She, should you need reminding, was Madison, the mermaid in *Splash!*; she was a somewhat unexpected astronomer in Steve Martin's Cyrano remake *Roxanne*, and if you seek something more gritty, she was in *Blade Runner* and *Kill Bill* and, since you need to know, *Attack of the 50ft Woman*.

I got involved in this lunatic trip because of a man I met in a pub. John Burton has a long, distinguished and exotic CV, but the first and most remarkable entry is Sunnyhill School.

At our first meeting, over pints in the White Horse, the topography of south London came into the conversation, and one or other of us revealed an unnatural familiarity with the postal district of SW16. Burton then talked of the days he spent Gerry-Durrelling round Biggin Wood, capturing hedgehogs and seeking birds' nests in a manner later and rightly considered reprehensible. But it was clear even then that Burton has had a taste for reprehensibility. It was this, allied with recklessness, that prompted him to assemble this extraordinary gathering of rainforest explorers.

He was at Sunnyhill a few years before me. Odd to think that Burton was doing for real what I was doing in my imagination: seeking out, contacting, living with wild creatures, touching the wild world. He has done much the same thing ever since. Not that Burton is eccentric. It's the rest of the world that's a bit peculiar. That became clear as pints became whiskies. He is also a scientist who never got round to collecting any qualifications, a musician with infinitely eclectic tastes, author of a remarkable number of books and a man whose every spare bit of wall is hung with paintings and drawings, almost all of them to do with wildlife. He says it is his ambition to die in as much debt as possible.

Here, then, is a classic British maverick. As a pioneer conservationist – he worked for the Natural History Museum, ran the Fauna and Flora Preservation Society and founded TRAFFIC, the organisation that monitors the trade in wildlife – he was by definition a maverick. But as conservation established its own orthodoxies, Burton became a maverick of the conservation movement. He founded the World Land Trust, an organisation conceived under the simple, brilliant, cut-to-the-chase, let's-do-the-show-right-here notion of saving endangered habitat by buying it. I don't think I am overdoing the filmic imagery here: after all, we have Darryl waiting to take an Amazonian step onstage.

David Tomlinson, the digi-scoper – one prone to taking photographs of birds by combining a digital camera and a telescope – has known Burton for years. He has spent most of his professional life working for *Country Life* magazine, and though a birder before all else, he chooses to play the part of the shootin' and fishin' squire, a role combined sporadically with that of the World War One subaltern. He is also keen on the arts of one-upmanship. He's an agreeable man in many ways, it must be said, and he has been a great supporter of the Trust. I had known him off and on for a good while myself.

Despite posing as a man o' the world, he is nothing of the kind. His Home Counties sensibilities were utterly confused by his arrival in the jungle with this crew of dazzling urbanites, none of whom would know an ocellated turkey from a wedge-tailed sabre-wing. This was puzzling for David, especially when you consider that the sabre-wing is a hummingbird and the turkey is, indeed, a turkey and genuinely enormous. He was still more confused about the nature of human sexuality. When we arrived at the field research centre, a pleasant place of wooden buildings in a forest glade, above which keel-billed toucans gave us a polychromatic welcome, we divvied up the rooms. I got Burton while David got lucky, and a room to himself.

The following morning, as David and I worked the forest edge with Vladimir Rodriguez, a Belizean field naturalist, while the fashionistas slept off their jet lag, he finally nerved himself to ask me the question that had been troubling him. "You know that make-up chap?"

"SJ, yes?"

"Well, I thought he was frightfully – you know – camp."

"Yes."

"But now he's sharing a room with a young lady!" I hadn't thought David's voice capable of reaching such a note.

"David," I said as gently as I could. "He is a young lady."

"Oh!" said David. "Oh… Oh."

Well, it was a confusing trip. That had to be admitted. Jaguar (cars) were involved because they like to be associated with real jaguars. *Hello!* magazine were involved, because they were paying for a photo-shoot of Darryl in the rainforest, plus a celeb interview. David and I were invited as wildlife writers, and it was hoped that all these – apparently quite contradictory – aims might mysteriously combine and bring about good things for the forest and the World Land Trust.

I was there because I have a passion for wildlife; SJ was there because he has a passion for Audrey Hepburn. Hepburn's cheekbones are not the subject you expect to discuss when you are staying in a hut in the jungle, but it is a subject that has consumed SJ since he was a boy. I have always been enthralled by passion, no matter what form it takes, and so I asked him over the dinner table on our first night about what mattered to him. SJ spoke his heart. It was clear right from the outset that he loved young ladies.

He was absolutely enraptured by the beauty of women. He had a Hepburn epiphany: "I realised right then that what I wanted to do was to help women look beautiful." Women did not strike a sexual response within him, but it was women that delighted him above all else in life. Mrs Watson would not have been impressed.

There was a little antipathy, a little wariness between David and the urbanites at first. But this dissipated quickly – in fact, as soon as he became overwhelmed by an ambition to take pictures of Darryl Hannah.

Darryl arrived with her gofer, Julie, and took up residence, but I shall spare you the details of how her room was prepared by all those with an interest in her comfort and good temper, especially Alison, the celeb writer, who filled the room with samples of all sorts of alternative beauty products in which she had an interest.

So enter Darryl. A strapping, handsome woman in her early 40s, blonde, strong face, worth a look, even two, but you wouldn't say: my God, she must be a film star. Perhaps that's what it's always like when you meet film stars. She was perfectly pleasant with everybody without trying to make conquests of us all; she was prepared to muck in; she felt a certain sense of privilege in being in the forest. She certainly didn't expect the forest to operate with Hollywood standards of cleanliness and freedom from insects. The only way you would realise that outside the forest she was a staggeringly famous person was in the matter of caution.

There was a natural holding-back of herself: something you get to recognise in people from whom everyone wants something. Even people who have never seen your movies want a little fix of your fame.

So the fashionista side of the party set to work at a ruined temple a short walk from camp: a photo-shoot for *Hello!*, with Nana clicking away, Alison flapping about and trying to seize control, while Emma from Jaguar spread massive waves of calm and SJ sought some magical combination of cosmetics that would not only enhance Darryl's already lovely face but stay on it for longer than two minutes.

In the rainforest, even film stars sweat: not in drops but in buckets. As we passed by looking for wildlife, I noticed that Darryl's legs bore trickles of blood from the mosquito bites, but she took this in her considerable stride. David, Vladi and I moved on and managed to get close encounters with Yucatan black howler monkey and Central American spider monkey, two great rainforest specialists. The spider monkeys climbed impossibly above us with the fifth limb giving them a convincingly arachnid appearance. The howlers keep in touch across the impenetrable thickness of the canopy by singing to each other. The first time I heard this song was from my bed: I thought for a long time that it was Burton snoring.

We switched camp, to a place by a lake. By this time the tension among the fashionistas had escalated alarmingly.

More than ever, Alison wanted control of everything that everyone was doing: with a bunch of anarchists like this, such an ambition was unrealistic to say the least. When not telling people what to do, Alison suffered. It was sad but true that every insect in the Belizean forest had a personal vendetta against her. She developed a limp from a bite on her ankle: would it never heal? The forest became her enemy. She wasn't happy. She wasn't mucking in. But she wanted her story all right, and what's more, she wanted it on her terms. This ambition made no one happy, herself least of all.

The one thing that really ate her up – apart from the insects, of course – was the feeling that *Hello!* might somehow be deprived of exclusivity. So she made it crystal clear that no one, no one at all, was to take any picture whatsoever of Darryl. To the subaltern inside David, this was a bugle-call to action. David, as a right-wing lover of freedom, at least his own, deeply resented this prohibition. No one was going to tell him what he could and couldn't photograph. So he whipped out his little digital camera and turned it not on birds but on Darryl. He kept sneaking up on the shoot to steal pictures. Alison grew apoplectic; David, at first considered an unassimilable outsider, was suddenly vastly popular.

David and I walked back from a spot of birding with Vladi and came on Darryl not preparing for a shoot or resting between sessions, but for once in the full rigour of action, action expressed here as a form of dramatic stillness. She was wearing a sarong, leaning on the jetty. The waters beyond her were spotted with hundreds and hundreds of little bird-houses on posts, homes for purple martins. Yet it was not the martins but Darryl that took the eye. She was unrecognisable from the comely woman I had already met. Here was a woman of quite staggering beauty.

This was not just a tribute to the mysteries of which SJ is a master. The beauty was beyond even his artistry, for you can't bring out what is not already there. This revelation of Darryl as a beauty of neck-wrenching iridescence was an extraordinary thing. For a start, it was an aspect of performance: a demonstration that beauty comes not just from bones and flesh and expression, but from the desire to be beautiful, the belief in your own beauty, from the knowledge that this was *show time* and so a show must be given.

It was the camera that made her beauty shine from within: take away the camera and the light would fade away. With the camera before her, Darryl, rock-still, was in flight. She looked pretty good in two dimensions, when I eventually saw the *Hello!* spread – but she was beyond-belief glorious in three. It was an extraordinary experience to be close to her when she really meant it: when she was prepared to release her inescapably mesmerising, till-then hidden qualities.

Most of us see most wildlife in two dimensions – on the television, in still pictures – and sometimes, it can look as lovely as Darryl as Roxanne, as fierce as Darryl in *Kill Bill*, as absurd as Darryl in *Splash!* But even then, all you see is the shadow on the wall of the cave. All you see is the pale memory of what has vanished. Me, I have been closer. I have shared three-dimensional space with some of the most remarkable beings on the planet; I have seen loveliness and ferocity and impossible wonder. But that is what I have chosen to look for. As SJ wanted to be close to female beauty, so I have chosen to be close to the beauty of the wild.

So close, indeed, that Burton was no longer speaking to me, or when he was doing so, he was having a job to ungrit his teeth. He had, even then, been to Belize, say 25 times on World Land Trust business. I should add here that the World Land Trust doesn't actually own any land in Belize, or anywhere in the world outside Britain, come to that. This is not a neo-colonial organisation. In Belize, the land is owned by the Belizean organisation, Programme for Belize. WLT helps to fund them, offers advice when required, is there always in support. As a result, in Belize there are 262,000 acres of rainforest safe from the destroyers; across the world there are 400,000 acres of endangered habitat that, because of the WLT, are not in any danger whatsoever. This, it became clearer every day that I spent in that forest, is a great organisation.

It is also one that functions to a very large extent on communication between partners. This works best on a one-on-one basis, between people who are both colleagues and friends. A shared aim presides over all that matters. Or perhaps I should say a shared love. The best kind of wild-life conservation has its basis in love. Love of the forest, love of its creatures, love of the wild is something you simply can't fake. I know: I share it, and when I meet people in the forest or out on the savannah, people I have never seen before, I know at once that there is a conversation, for there is always a conversation when you have a big thing in common. And what we have in common is love. So it was that Burton was in yet another meeting with friends/colleagues when David and I made a trip into the forest with Vladi.

And I am deeply sorry to say, deeply ashamed to say that we stole Burton's love from him. Perhaps it is true to say that we usurped the privilege of the love he had borne longer and deeper than either of us. Burton is a mammal-man before anything else. He is there to save the forests: he is also there to savour them, for his ambition to save these places has its basis in love. In this tract of Belizean forest, he, more than any other single person on the planet, has caused it to continue existing, and with it, all the creatures that have their being there. But he was denied the fruits of that love, and these were, foolishly, recklessly and capriciously, given to me instead. I've been trying to repay him ever since.

All the same, I am glad that I was not offered a choice before the trip. If anyone had said to me, what would you like better, to see a jaguar, or to kiss Darryl Hannah? there is only one choice a red-blooded male could make, and I'd have been sad to miss the kiss. But I am getting ahead of myself. There, walking down the road, in glistening, rippling, muscling, maculated perfection, was a jaguar: *el tigre*: the mammal that everyone who comes to New World forests wants to see and which so few do. Burton, in all those trips, never got so lucky. Vladi had only seen 16 jaguars in six years in the forest. This was not a privilege I had earned: but one I had a duty to cherish.

It was the perfect evening for a night's crocodiling. The lagoon before the field station was a great place for Morelet's crocodile, a species that loves the fresh waters of the Yucatan peninsular. We set off by boat once night had fallen, and by dint of good luck and masterful shoving, I found myself sitting next to Darryl. Now I have a gambit that can hold women of a certain sort fascinated for hours. I am a horseman, I keep horses at home and horse-talk captivates me. "Tell me about your horses, Darryl."

So she was off: she had some rescue horses, all with long flowing tales attached, and she told me them all: their individual stories and their individual charms of character. We talked the horse-talk with great delight as we chugged over the silent black lake, spotlighting for crocs. The

Morelet's don't get big, not by the standards of the Nile crocs of the Luangwa River, but they can still reach eight feet long and it's better not to pick a fight with them.

Darryl, it soon became clear, had a powerful and totally unfocused love for animals and for the wild world. She spoke in a breathless, slightly girly voice that was rather at odds with her heftiness. "Are they really blind?" she asked as a bat made a millimetre-exact pass over our heads. At one stage she fished a drowning moth from the water and attempted to dry it out and restore it to life. The attention she gave this was for a while all-consuming. I watched in fascination for some time, and then asked, perhaps unfeelingly: "Why don't you try mouth-to-mouth?"

"Moth-to-moth?"

And then she was telling me of her encounter with wolves. She had a friend who was making a wildlife documentary, and he had a wolf pack staked out. Darryl begged permission to get close to these wolves, and no doubt bowled over by the full Darryl charm, the friend agreed: "But you must just observe. Don't do anything but observe. Right?"

So Darryl waited and waited and eventually the wolves appeared: "And I couldn't help it, I just got down on all fours and said: 'Here doggy! Here doggy!'

"And the lead one came up to me and sniffed and I just kept real still and then he took hold of my lower lip between his teeth, and then he gave it a little shake. And then he led everyone off."

Darryl, it seemed, has a genuine affinity for non-human life, of a somewhat unconventional kind. She was prepared to risk everything – as SJ will tell you, looks are quite important for a film star and there is not much work for beauties with savaged lips – for a chance encounter with a wolf. And I thought well, if the wolf is howling, the Darryl is barking. I also thought her extremely wonderful as we chugged side by side across the black lake. We found our croc too, a six-footer that stayed in the light for a good few minutes, passing right under the boat, before eventually disappearing into the depths. And so we returned through the black Belizean night: Burton trying to buy up the entire world, Tomlinson with his little camera and his telescope, SJ with his make-up, Alison with her notes and her ailments, Darryl with her lupine memories and her dead moth, me. As mad a ship as ever I have sailed on.

Darryl cheek-kissed farewell with us all, and said it had been an unforgettable trip. She wanted to be deeply involved with the WLT, but nothing came of it. Alison's piece made *Hello!*, and Nana's pictures (and Darryl's face) looked gorgeous. Emma had a damascene experience, resolved to work for conservation instead of the luxury market, and now does the PR work for the WLT. Nana, also enthralled, contributes pictures for the WLT whenever she can. SJ moved into event management, and is planning a big one for the WLT. David went back to the

Home Counties a more worldly man. And me, I was asked to become a council member for the WLT, and have done my bit for this remarkable organisation ever since.

22. Badger
Meles meles

I have written about sport for *The Times* since 1982. Sport is part of my life. I talk sport all the time, by way of business, or for the fun of it: the new England cricket captain will do a great job, or maybe he won't; the new England football manager hasn't got a clue, or maybe he has. These conversations are part of my life: they're an important part of the way many people relate. It is one of the great male traditions: your friend's wife has just left him, so you take him to the pub and talk about Arsenal. It also tends to be one of those things that pass from father to son: to this day, my father and I energetically talk cricket and rugby.

We played cricket in the garden when I was young and still thought my father could play; he eventually turned out both for and against the cricket team I co-founded, when I still thought I could play. When it was my turn for fatherhood, I made sure Joe had bats and balls as soon as he could walk. His response from the earliest age was to ignore the bat and toss the ball into a bush. Then he got on with something interesting. Eddie, however, loves a ball, and we have invented a number of curious games that suit his take on the world. Throwing the ball up and down the stairs is a favourite, and there are strange garden games that involve the slide and the bushes, or best, a precipitous bank. He stands at the top with me at the bottom and throws at me forcefully and ambidextrously and occasionally accurately.

But Joe has never played a ball game in his life. Energetic and crazed movements on the trampoline have given him pleasure across the years, but the idea that anyone could enjoy kicking a ball or catching it baffles him entirely. He has never watched a second of televised sport of his own volition. I watch a fair bit: when Joe catches me at it, he politely walks away. These things no more involve him than a discussion of *Finnegans Wake*. I have occasionally attempted to explain it to him – sport rather than the Wake – and though he has listened amiably enough, it is clear that sport will never touch him. He is mildly intrigued that this rum stuff absorbs me: but sport is something we will never share.

He looks a bit like me, with a long bony face. He has

long hair, as I do, which he ties back, as I do. He is home-schooled, being a natural not-fitter-inner: I was self-employed for 24 years, so I can relate to that. On the other hand, at 15 he is six foot three, already six inches taller than me.

He doesn't read much, which saddens me. Narrative enthrals him, as it has always enthralled me, but not so much in book form. I read him all The Chronicles of Narnia and then the Harry Potter series until he was old enough to read them for himself, so that was something. I read him *My Family and Other Animals* two or three times. He loves comedy. When he was nine, he discovered *Dad's Army*: I purchased the entire series and it kept us going for months; years, really: we watched the lot and then watched it all over again, and we still watch favourite episodes. We share other ancient sitcoms – *The Good Life* is a favourite – and some carefully selected modern comedians. Laughter and narrative: great things.

He has talents I don't begin to understand, still less possess. For some years he made thrilling models of animals in clay, with a natural sense of proportion and drama. He makes model stage sets for *Doctor Who* and *Torchwood*, initially from cardboard boxes, more recently from plywood. He has a natural dexterity that is utterly foreign to me: a love of practical solutions that leaves me bemused. He recently completed a scale model of the moon-buggy from the James Bond film *Diamonds Are Forever*. The tricky thing was the wheels; he eventually mastered them with a soldering iron. I have never soldered anything in my life, nor will I. He uses these sets and props for animated films, and they tend to end with the whole lot going up in flames. The stars are plastic figures that he creates himself. He buys conventional figures and transforms them with knife and putty and paint. As a virtuoso piece of work, he created Bertie Bassett, the Liquorice Allsorts man, out of a figure of Batman. Inevitably, he can also do extraordinary things with a computer, and uses these baffling skills for his tales and his videos. He now devotes himself to the guitar with an extraordinary passion.

All this is quite beyond me. The story, the cliff hangers, the jokes, the imagination: all this I can relate too. But to see him paint the smile on the face of the Joker with a paintbrush three hairs thick is something that makes me say: who is this guy? What on earth has he got to do with me? What on earth is fatherhood, what does it mean, what kind of legacy is this, a son who towers over my head and makes working cars and animated films?

Parenthood is a perpetual compromise between neglect and pushing. The last thing you want to do with anything that matters to you – art, books, wildlife – is to ram it down their throats, as the process is always called. I didn't try to ram animals down Joe's throat, but the first word he spoke was bird. I started taking him to the zoo as soon as he was able to deal with it. There are a lot of bad things said about zoos, and I've said some of them myself: that they don't celebrate the animals, they celebrate the cages, that the subject is not wildlife but bars, that they don't teach about our kinship with our fellow-animals but the barriers we erect between them and us.

But if that's the lesson zoos are supposed to teach, it was just one more lesson that Joe didn't pay attention to. Right from the first, as other families hustled past at high speed – "I don't think much of that!" "He isn't even moving!" – Joe would settle down for a good long gaze, silent and absorbed. I told him about a survey done at Antwerp Zoo, in which it seemed as if the researchers were working on the famous chimp colony. In fact, they were working on the visitors. The most frequent remark they recorded was "I could watch them all day". The average length of stay was one minute. Joe laughed at this: and settled down to watch, to seek an involvement, to establish a belonging.

When I was young, I sought the wild through books and through the imagination. Joe had the real thing. Cautiously, anxious at all costs to avoid the dreaded ramming-down-throat scenario, I introduced him to accessible wild things. Gradually, we acquired a double pattern: that of relishing the wildlife all around us, the sort of thing casually encountered in the garden or on journeys, and that of making expeditions to enjoy special things. We have been to Africa, to the Luangwa Valley, of course, to see the great beasts. We went to Slovakia to find bears. And we have made other, shorter journeys. I have shown him the wild, and we have done things together that, when I was his age, I had believed were for ever beyond my scope. Joe enjoys the occasional morning's birding at Minsmere, without getting too obsessive about identification. If he undertakes these trips in a small way to humour me, then I am honoured. Mammals touch him more deeply. We have been to look at the red deer rut, and walked among the belling stags and the coolly assessing hinds. We have watched foxes at play, we have watched water voles at swim. All this I do to enjoy the moment, the expedition and the companionship: and yet, I can't quite stamp out the spark of fatherly ambition, the hope that each trip is an experience that will keep him interested in wildlife for the rest of his life, that will, by no means incidentally, give us something to share for as long as I'm around to share things. Naturally I want him to enjoy wildlife: how could I not wish him one the greatest joys available to humankind?

But of course, I also want to have stuff we can enjoy together, and in this, I suppose that I am seeking some kind of confirmation that he is, at heart, ever so slightly like me: that the something of me in him can show itself in a way that brings us both joy. It's a rum and complex business, but anyway, he was unambiguously pleased when I suggested that we spend an evening badgering. It's something we had done a couple of times before, the first time when he was no older than ten. Both times, the badgers came, we had our reward and it was all great. But now he was 14, absurdly tall and with more and more complicated teenager things in his life.

So I organised a visit to a badger hide set up by the Suffolk Wildlife Trust, and when we arrived we took a pot of peanuts from the stash provided and cast them in front of the little hut. The hide is a comfortably appointed place set up for long vigils, and we entered and began to wait as the light started to change. We sat behind sealed windows: it was not just our shapes we needed to conceal, it was also our smell.

But a bad thing happened as we closed the door and took our places. Someone raced an engine flat out, screaming it, again and again, for a sustained period, maybe five minutes, the sound ripping apart the mild Suffolk air. It was enough to keep any sane animal hunkered down and out of sight for hours.

So we sat. We sat, gazing out at the small patch of wood that lay beyond the sealed windows. It was – and I had plenty of time to think about this – a place odd to human eyes, one where no paths exist, which has no human logic, which a human can only cross with a scramble and a fall and stinging. Even a scrap of English woodland is wilder than we know. Below us, in the voluptuously diggable earth, we could see the great ramparts of a badger's palace:

a grand project that had continued for years from one generation to the next, a great narrative told in friable earth. And the light faded and we saw the odd bunny, and once a rat. We heard the sudden scream of a jay. We ate sandwiches. I drank a can of beer, Joe drank a bottle of water. We exchanged a couple of remarks in whispers. A joke, a muffled laugh. Occasionally I shifted position, or Joe did. The light was almost gone. There was a rather perfunctory dusk chorus. I was beginning to prepare in my mind the right sort of thing to say: well, that's wild animals for you. They're not tame, you know. That's the point, eh? We'll try another time, but there it is, we'll put this one down to experience. Sorry it's been a bit of a disappointment, but hey, that's wildlife. Hoping that even after this wasted evening, he'd give the wild another chance.

It's a big thing for a teenage boy to sit in silence and stillness for three hours. It's a big thing for a teenager to have anything at all to do with the wild, for the years of adolescence are a time – there is even research to prove it – when you are at your least responsive to the non-human world. The need to establish a social identity and a personal view of life takes up all your energy. For most people, the years of your teens are the lost years of the wild: the years when tamelife dominates everything that you do, to the exclusion of things even slightly wild.

Come, I thought. We'll give it another 15 minutes. I

glanced over to Joe. He won't be able to take much more, I thought. And then, like an angel appearing in answer to a prayer, a big stripy nose emerged from the earth: a creature as improbable as any I have seen in my life. The badger that appeared in front of us looked almost absurdly like Mr Badger of *The Wind in the Willows*. It is when I see a badger that I am most conscious of the inseparable nature of the wild world and the world of the imagination.

A second badger appeared, and then a third. We could hear them snuffling, for badgers are great snufflers, as they hoovered up peanuts in the most tremendous hurry, as if the long wait after the roaring of the engine had given them an appetite. The pear-shaped bodies, the immensely powerful back end, the corpulent grace, a little like that of sumo wrestlers: these are creatures made for the earth. It was now almost dark, but our long staring had given us our night vision, and we could make out the badgers from the flashing of the white on their faces, so dazzlingly set off by the black stripes. Is that what the stripes are for: for nocturnal signalling? And then they vanished, each one in a different direction, foraging, munching, revelling in the night, the dark: each one knowing that he had the sett and each other to return to. A badger is a very secure animal: top predator, a full social life, and everything based around the monumental diggings, the great underground castles.

So we left, taking our rubbish, locking up, leaving the

key and the empty peanut pot in the right place, and returned home. "Sorry we had such a long wait."

"That's all right."

"I thought they wouldn't come."

"I thought they probably would."

"I was getting a speech ready about... Never mind, that's wildlife."

"Why?"

23. Barn owl
Tyto alba

When I was ten I won a Highly Commended certificate in a poetry competition that involved, I think, the entire borough of Wandsworth, or at least, the primary schools therein. It was the peak of my achievement as a poet, though I carried on gamely for another dozen years.

His eyesight keen
Scans round the green
The owl is out to kill

The vermin take cover
At his deadly hover
The owl is out to kill

A careless rat wanders astray
The owl is down without delay
The owl has got his kill

I think we can all agree that Highly Commended was generous in the circumstances. But I include these all-too-mortal lines as proof that the barn owl had always haunted me.

It is almost the literal truth: for barn owls are ghost-birds, wraith-birds, spook-owls, traditionally associated with fading light, pale birds with baby faces that come into being with the gathering dark, crossing the countryside on soundless wings, living in abandoned dwellings; birds with a taste for ruins, whose un-bird-like, un-man-like, un-living-thing-like screech signals the arrival of the night and the time of fear.

Barn owls were my passion. I knew I would never see one, any more than I would see a unicorn, but the haunting of my imagination was as meaningful to me as the haunting of any buildings. There was a photograph that helped a great deal with the haunting process.

It was, like the marsh harrier picture mentioned earlier, taken by the great primordial bird photographer Eric Hosking, a man who was to lose his eye to an owl that resented his presence, though this was a tawny, not a barn. Hosking called his autobiography *An Eye For A Bird*.

The image, captured in 1934, became a classic: a flat white human face, sphinx-like, Buddha-like, as wise or as sinister as human imagination could make it, carrying in its beak a careless rat; or, to be more accurate, a careless short-tailed field vole. The face human, the wings angelic, the appetite bestial: what more does the imagination need to feed on?

But for me, barn owls were never sinister. I rather prided myself on that. They were part of the natural world, and if they made a spooky call, that was not because barn owls were spooks but because humans tended to get spooked. If the life of a barn owl is alien to our own, then it is the more to be cherished. For me, the fascination of barn owls lay not in their supernatural possibilities, in an anthropomorphic understanding of their natures, in fear, in superstition, in anything at all to do with imposed human ideas: no, my imagination was fired by the thought of these pale silent killers leading their serious lives remote from human understanding.

At one stage of my childhood, I designed my own coat of arms. I had a brief craze on heraldry and learned all the magic words and some of the magical meaning of the bend or baton sinister, the stag trippant attired, the eagle displayed, the lion rampant gules. I prepared my escutcheon with some care, ready for the day when I was given a knighthood by an admiring monarch: argent, a fess gules, in chief three barn owl heads proper. Barn owls for their beauty, barn owls for my imagination, barn owls for Barnes. I never thought I'd ever see a real one.

When I returned from my time in Asia and started going to places richer in possibilities than Streatham

Common, I made a number of jaunts with my friend Tim, a decent birder who took me to some fine places just a short train ride from London. "What will we see, Tim?" "Oh, chance of black tern on the reservoir, maybe golden plover on the moor, don't think it's cold enough for smew... short-eared owl is almost definite... big wader numbers... diving duck... and turning home, we might pick up a barn owl in the dusk."

Oh yes, might pick up a unicorn, might pick up a hippogriff, might bump into a sphinx and get asked the odd riddle. Might meet the creature of my dreams, might meet the creature that, above all others, haunted the imagination of my childhood, might meet the most beautiful, most impossible creature that ever took wing. But we never did.

When I was researching my Minsmere book, I had been told that barn owls were frequently to be seen above the Minsmere Levels: that if I looked out across the water from Island Mere Hide at dusk, I would almost certainly see one. And so I looked. Again and again, and for extended periods, I stared across the lovely lake, trying to coax a fleck of white into the greying sky. Impossibly distant, looking beyond the ducks and the swans, staring at a place too far for intimacy. Still, just a glimpse, just a brief appearance of a distant pale bird would be a start. Eventually, I was granted just that: yes, a white bird; yes, on arched wings; yes, unquestionably a barn owl. Not because I could recognise it, but because it could not be anything else: it was a negative encounter, though not without its beauty. It wasn't a sighting that brought me knowledge or understanding: just a rather piquant detail on a lovely painting: a pale wash of sky with a still paler brushstroke: on a field argent an owl argent, tantalising, teasing, thrilling enough in its way: it was a sight that increased the appetite rather than satisfied it.

Cind and I spent a good deal of time in Suffolk while I was researching the book, and when I had finished, Suffolk refused to let us go. There were elements of a homecoming for Cind, though it was a home she had never lived in: the barge-sailing side of her family comes from the Shotley peninsular. The Suffolk coast is something of an acquired taste: the bleakness, even in summer, can be disturbing, and it is marked by strange patches which are certainly not the sea, but are not entirely land either. But Suffolk became our place.

It was just after Christmas, and we had decided to take a few bracing days of big skies and winter waders, walks and pub meals, whisky by the fire and giggling runs into icy sheets.

We took a walk in the afternoon around the Alde estuary: a place of casual immensities and the same pearly light that you get in Venice. No coincidence: it's the light of brackish lagoons, but here, instead of Tintoretto and Carpaccio, we had avocets and marsh harrier. Reeds like a field of corn, sabled water, argent sky. And a miracle.

There before us, just a few yards away, like the richest gift ever bestowed, a barn owl. A barn owl proper. He was working the rough land beneath a grove of recently planted trees, perched on a pink square tree-guard and gravely surveying the rank grass beneath. We watched as he flew to another. And another. It was as if we had been given the gift not only of barn owl but of invisibility. Occasionally he dropped onto the grass. Silent, always silent, for the wings of an owl are muffled with feathers. This is not just so that the prey animals can't hear him coming: it also means that his hearing has no interference. A barn owl locates his prey by listening: the sound of his own progress would spoil that. His ears are placed asymmetrically so that he can get a cross-bearing: he can plunge with confidence onto a field vole he has never seen. It's not his eyesight keen that matters after all: it's his ear-hearing keen. His earsight, perhaps. No wonder I was only Highly Commended.

We watched the owl until dusk fell, for getting on for an hour, agog, almost bewildered by the sense of privilege. Then we went back to our rented cottage, knowing that Suffolk had, with this transcendental vision of the barn owl, established an eternal claim over us. We would be back here as often as we could, despite all the things that kept us anchored to the rim of London.

Five or six years later, our house was the epicentre of

an owl chorus such as I had never heard before. It was early autumn, a time of great movements. Young owls, parted from their parents, go out to seek their fortunes: sometimes they attempt to invade a place already taken. They make enquiries: these are answered, often with great force. All these matters are discussed in sound. On this night, all these autumnal quests and movements and challenges seemed to happen at once. The excitement they generated stimulated every owl within hearing distance – within earsight, perhaps – no matter what his species. It was cold, but we opened all the windows of the downstairs room we were in, leaning out to try and establish number and direction, to make some kind of sense of this barrage of sound. The nearest I could come up with was seven or eight little owls, four or five barn owls and two or three tawnies. The little owls yelped. The tawnies alternated their own sounds, the wavering hoot of horror films and the sharp, dissyllabic contact call. And every so often, the barn owls gave out that extraordinary hissing roar.

We had only just moved in. For all I knew we would hear this wild chorus every year, perhaps every night in season. But no: it was a one-off: a strange coincidence of birds and night and excitement. Harry Potter had not been written, and Joe, then only three, was yet to fall under his spells, but it was a little like being in Privet Drive in the opening pages of the first book. Owls beyond computation: what message did they carry for us?

For now, we had moved to Suffolk and I learned almost at once that we were now in the land of the barn owl. I began to live with barn owls in terms of casual intimacy. Birds that had been fantastical creatures, mythical beings given life by my imagination, were now daily companions. I saw barn owls when walking the dog, first when she was a puppy prone to wild runs and flopping falls, now when she is a dignified old lady with an increasing taste for short cuts. I saw barn owls when I went looking for other birds. I saw barn owls when I worked with my horses. I saw barn owls from the windows of the house. I was able to recognise them from the smallest clue: a distant pale shape following the line of a hedge: a half-glimpse of the effortful, floppy wing: the somehow immensely satisfying moment when a barn owl perches, closes its pale wings and disappears, its brown mantle blending instantly with the background. The sound of their presence was always with us. They were not so frequent as to be unremarkable: they were not so infrequent as to be a surprise. They were there as a permanent validation, if you like, a proof that my imagination and the real wild world had achieved some kind of unity.

There is a barn owl box in a big oak a short way behind the house. Barn owls have roosted there. Stock doves have also bred there instead: and here, you have to put on a serious face and explain that stock doves, being amber-listed worldwide, are in greater danger than barn owls and are therefore More Important. I can't say that I wouldn't prefer a family of barn owls: still, the place is there if they ever need it. Barn owls have also roosted in my barn, and left their horribly turd-like pellets on the floor.

They are on the increase in this part of Suffolk, because farmers are increasingly inclined (and subsidised) to leave areas of rough grassland where an owl can hunt for careless, short-tailed field voles, and also because the Suffolk Wildlife Trust has gone to some trouble to persuade landowners to put up barn owl boxes. With the destruction of old barns and tumbledown outbuildings, the owls have become homeless. Hollow trees that they would annex in a world without humans tend to be cut down impatiently, though two or three fields away, there is just such a tree, a venerable oak, and though the farmer has been itching for his power-saw for years, his wife won't let him touch it. And it generally has barn owls within. There is a change taking place in the way the world understands barn owls: they were once seen as spooks and evil omens, then they were (wrongly) cast as pheasant-eating villains, but now they are admired, desired and prestigious.

Barn owls define our Suffolk lives. Joe has been familiar with them since he was at nursery school. Eddie can recognise them: he can sign them, making Biggles-goggles with his fingers, and say "barn owl" distinctly. Important words to master, I think.

Here, Cind and I have known joys and suffered

sadness. Here, Joe and Eddie have done and are doing their growing up. Outside, there's lots and lots of Suffolk: and every so often, a barn owl. If you miss one, there'll be another along soon enough, like the 49 bus that used to take me from Streatham to the Natural History Museum. I have written a lot of words in this house, pausing often to look away from my desk and out of the window. It's not the best vantage point of the house, and barn owls are unusual at my desk, rather like inspiration. Like a barn owl, it best comes unexpected, the better to be treasured. My tamelife has always been punctuated and illustrated and spelt and narrated by my wildlife; these days there are times when the two things have at last become indistinguishable.